CASE STUDIES IN
CULTURAL ANTHROPOLOGY

GENERAL EDITORS
George and Louise Spindler
STANFORD UNIVERSITY

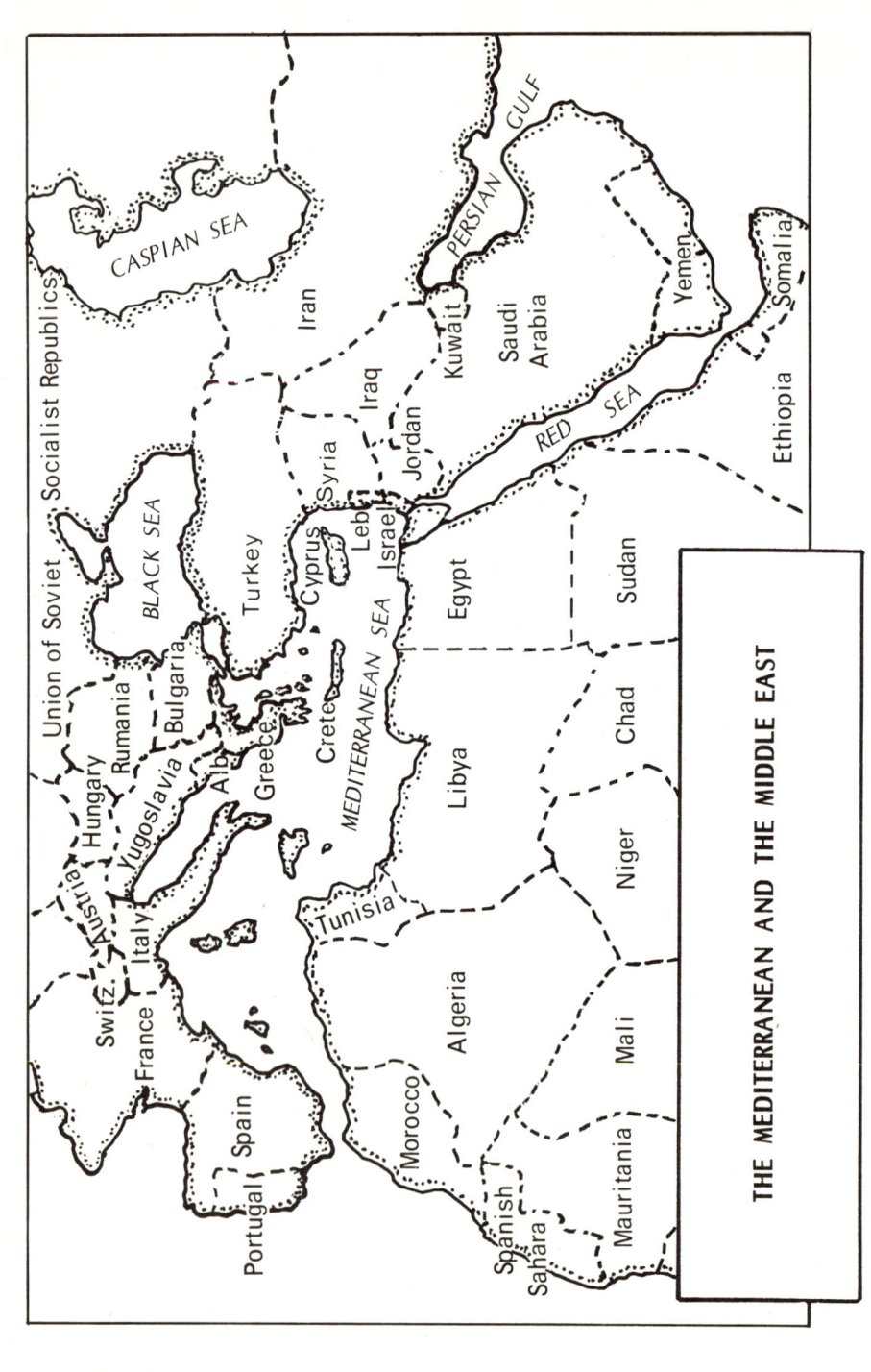

THE WALLS OF ACRE

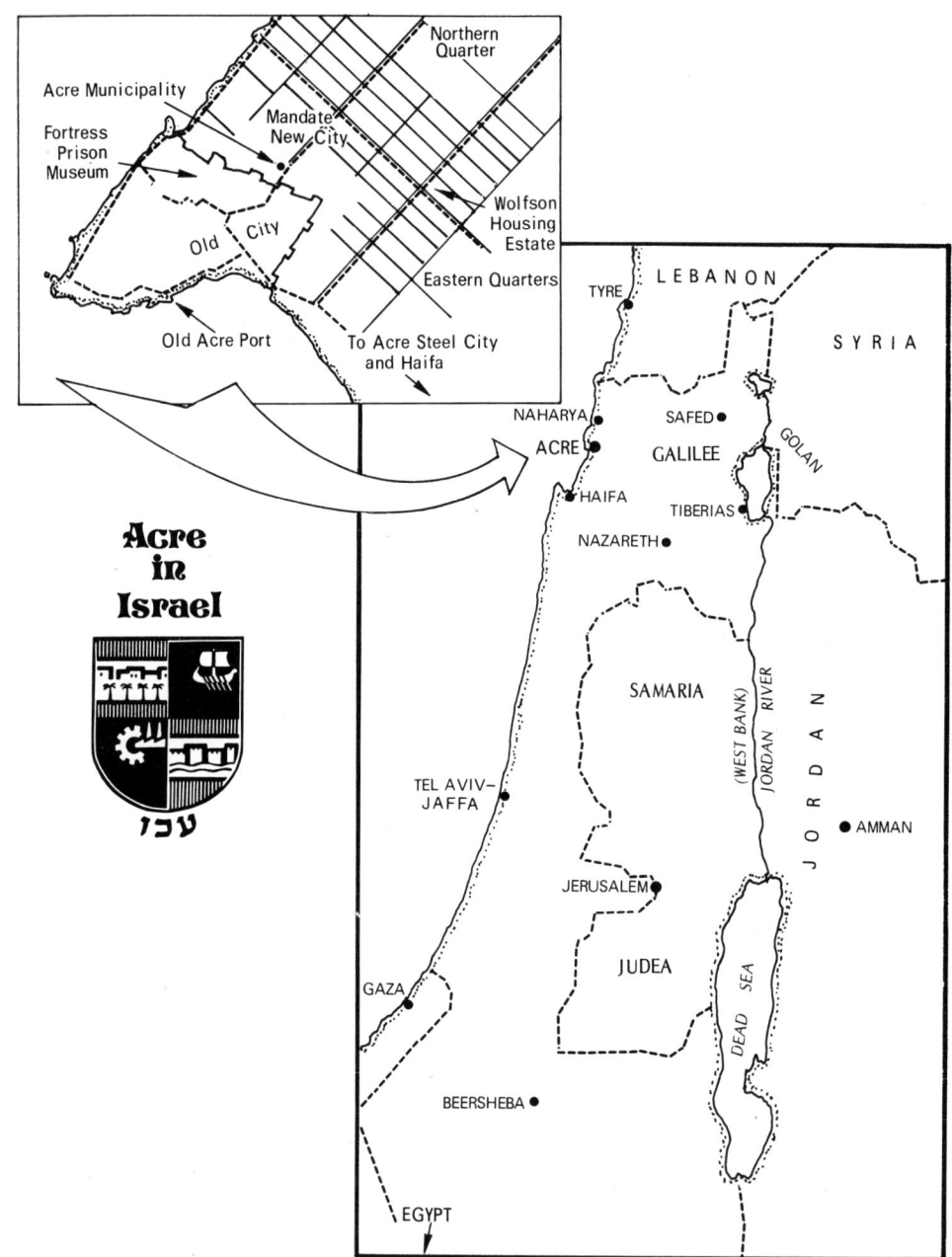

THE WALLS OF ACRE
Intergroup Relations and Urban Development in Israel

By
MORTON RUBIN
Northeastern University

HOLT, RINEHART AND WINSTON, INC.
NEW YORK   CHICAGO   SAN FRANCISCO   ATLANTA
DALLAS   MONTREAL   TORONTO   LONDON   SYDNEY

Library of Congress Cataloging in Publication Data
Rubin, Morton, 1923-
 The walls of Acre
 (Case studies in cultural anthropology)
 Bibliography: p. 135
 1. Acre, Israel—Social conditions.
2. Social interactions. 3. Social group—Case studies.
 I. Title. II. Series.
HN761.P33A37   301.11'07'22   74-8726
ISBN: 0-03-086299-X

Copyright © 1974 by Holt, Rinehart and Winston, Inc.

All rights reserved

Printed in the United States of America

4 5 6 7 8   059   9 8 7 6 5 4 3 2 1

In Honor of John Philip Gillin
and His Generation

Foreword

About the Series

These case studies in cultural anthropology are designed to bring to students, in beginning and intermediate courses in the social sciences, insights into the richness and complexity of human life as it is lived in different ways and in different places. They are written by men and women who have lived in the societies they write about and who are professionally trained as observers and interpreters of human behavior. The authors are also teachers, and in writing their books they have kept the students who will read them foremost in their minds. It is our belief that when an understanding of ways of life very different from one's own is gained, abstractions and generalizations about social structure, cultural values, subsistence techniques, and the other universal categories of human social behavior become meaningful.

About the Author

Morton Rubin is Professor of Sociology at Northeastern University in Boston, his native home. He began rural community field research in western Europe during World War II and extended this experience through doctoral study in the Modern Culture of the South under the direction of the late Dr. John P. Gillin at the University of North Carolina. The dissertation was published as *Plantation County* in 1951 by the University of North Carolina Press.

In 1950, Dr. Rubin made the first of several trips to Israel, where he worked for the Israeli Ministry of Social Welfare and involved himself in the comparative study of immigrant community organization, intergroup relations, and urban development processes. The city of Acre serves as a special case encompassing all of these interests.

Dr. Rubin has been a member of the Departments of Sociology and Anthropology at the University of Wisconsin and Northeastern University. He has undertaken surveys of American Negro rural-urban migration and neighborhood response to such public programs as urban renewal. Recently he reported a series of case studies of *Organized Citizen Participation in Boston*, sponsored by the National League of Cities and the U.S. Department of Housing and Urban Development for the Boston Urban Observatory. He is currently evaluating public policy in the metropolitan environment.

x   FOREWORD

About the Book

Acre, Israel, is an ancient city that reflects in its history and its present condition the turbulent past and present of the Middle East. It has been occupied by many different peoples and powers and, particularly during the Crusades, was ruined and rebuilt more than once. It was a site in the famous movie "Exodus." Today it plays a key symbolic role in Jewish-Arab relations and reflects the great tensions between these two peoples and cultures. It is also a site of urban and industrial development that reflects worldwide trends as well as the determination of the state of Israel to survive and progress—to provide a homeland for dispersed Jews and to find solutions to the disaffection of the Arab minority within the country.

Acre today is a city that contains many diverse elements. The majority of the Jewish population is not of a single kind. There are European, African, and Asian Jews, and an Israeli-born generation is emerging with its own cultural values. There are also several Christian denominations as well as Muslim sects among the Arabs. Townsmen, peasants, and bedouins have found in Acre a place to market in times of peace and a place for refuge in times of war.

Acre is a strategic site within which to observe and interpret intergroup relations. The author has, understandably, made this a major focus of the case study, but he does a great deal more. After giving us a substantial overview of the history of the region, the features of urban development, and some understanding of the extraordinarily intricate ethnic and religious composition of the city, he moves to the level of daily life and of individuals. He also describes the ceremonial round which, like the contingents it represents, is complex. He concludes with an analysis of community identity, using the emblem of Acre, reproduced as a frontispiece for this case study, as the focus of his symbolic analysis.

The case study moves far beyond the oversimplifications of the Israeli-Arab relationship that one gathers from mass media. The total situation is seen as combinations of parts within wholes. The tensions that are suffered today on both sides cannot be seen merely as the result of machinations by evil men. They are the result of historical forces, and the needs of people seeking to develop identity and enhance pride. The case study does not attempt to deal with the entire Israeli-Arab relationship. It is concerned primarily with Acre, Israel, where intergroup relations are a daily fact of life. Within the city it appears that there are pragmatic and viable bases for communication, however tenuous they may be.

GEORGE AND LOUISE SPINDLER
General Editors

Phlox, Wisconsin

Preface

This cultural case study of Acre, Israel, is based on my four field trips over the past two decades and on documentary sources. The result is an indepth evaluation of intergroup relations and a study of the latest developmental period of a city that is four thousand years old.

The Israeli Ministry of Social Welfare sponsored my first visit to Acre on a weekend early in 1952, when I was conducting a survey of community services for the United Nations. In Acre's Old City the American Friends Service Committee had established a community center, primarily for Arab refugees from the 1948 Arab-Israeli War. We were developing a theoretical framework for actual intergroup relations and service at the local level.

During 1954 I was able to sojourn in Acre's Old City while on a Visiting Fellowship from Princeton University's Center of International Studies. I sought to discover the meaning of "community" to Middle Easterners in terms of culture and institutions. I paid special attention to the impact of modern industrialization and nationalism, and noted that traditional kinship and ethnic values were giving way to new forms of class and status.

It became possible to spend most of the year 1965 in Acre's Old and New Cities. I had Sabbatical leave from Northeastern University and a travel grant-in-aid from the Middle East Committee of the Social Science Research Council. This time I focused on public and private activities of Acre's residents and their responses to national and international events.

My fourth trip to Acre took place in 1968, the purpose of which was to assess the consequences of the Six-Day War. Most economic and political life seemed to continue its daily course. But social relations and psychological identification had become polarized by the Arab Palestinian and Jewish Zionist causes. Acre's explosive situation seemed to test the limits of community.

Several esteemed colleagues have given me encouragement during these several years of urban cultural observation and analysis in Acre. Gratitude is herewith expressed to Roland L. Warren, John Gulick, S. Frederick Seymour, Charles Tilly, Catherine Bateson, and Sami Geraisy. My dear wife, Elizabeth, and sons, Joel and David, have provided companionship as well as friendly and cogent criticism. Toni Emrich and Elyce Misher have provided valuable editorial assistance. Dr. George Spindler has urged me on to higher levels of instructional communication. Above all, this work is dedicated to the people of Acre, Israel, who provide a living example of survival in the aftermath of war while developing ways of personal growth in the pursuit of well-being.

MORTON RUBIN

Boston, Massachusetts
May 1974

Contents

Foreword	ix
Preface	xi
Prologue	xvii
Introduction: Perceptions of Site and Situation	1
1. Region and Locality: Crossroads and Mosaic	5
The City of Acre in Regional Context 5	
Ancient and Classical Periods 6	
Under Caliphates and Crusaders 8	
The Turkish Period 9	
Acre under the British Mandate for Palestine 12	
2. A Development City in Israel	15
The Arab-Israeli War and Its Aftermath 15	
The First Stages of Development 17	
The Role of Strong Leadership 23	
Limitations to Growth 26	
3. The Arab Minority	29
Public Life 30	
Home Life and Family 32	
Communalism as Unity amidst Diversity 35	
The Muslim-Arab Community 36	
Christian Arab Communities 39	
Individual Adaptation and Mobility 42	
Increased Arab Alienation since 1967 45	
4. Ashkenazi Jews from Europe	49
Refugees from the Holocaust 50	
Ethnic Linkages and Differences 52	
New Alignments through Religious Action 53	
Localism and Mobility 55	
5. Sephardi-Oriental Jews from Muslim Lands	61
Oriental Communalism in Transition 63	
Secularizing Tendencies 66	

xiv CONTENTS

    Bridge versus Marginality   68
    The "Other" Israel and New Reference Groups   71

6. Daily Life and Normative Roles   77
    Early Morning   77
    Off to Work   80
    Domestic Duties   83
    Youth Culture   86

7. Ceremonial Rounds   93
    Minority Religious Communal Links   93
    Muslim Festivals   94
    Christian Festivals   96
    Jewish Religious Festivals Reinforce Zionism   99
    Labor Celebrates May Day   102
    National Identity Problems on Israeli Independence Day   103
    The Integrating Aspects of Elections   104
    Community Welfare Extension   107

8. Achieving Community Identity   111
    Economic Adaptation through Acre Steel City   112
    Intergroup Relations at the Wolfson Housing Estate   113
    Intergenerational Integration through the Fortress Prison Museum   115
    Development Plans for the Seaport   116
    The Functions of Community   119

Appendixes   123
    A. Selected Chronology Influencing the History of Acre   123
    B. Voting for the Israeli National Assembly and the Acre
        Municipal Council 1969 and 1973   127
    C. Selective Population Facts: City of Acre   129

Glossary   131

Recommended Reading   135

Additional References   139

THE WALLS OF ACRE

Prologue

The world's attention has once more been drawn to events in Israel and the Middle East. The region has become a crucible of nationalist conflict for the fourth time since the end of World War II. The outbreak of hostilities in October 1973, on the Jewish holy day of Yom Kippur and the Muslim festival of Ramadan, reinforces the sense of incompatibility between Hebrew and Arab nationalistic claims.

Israel has been caught off balance by Egyptian and Syrian military assertiveness and the support of major powers. Israel's feelings of isolation have led to a chastisement of its Labor leadership in postwar elections. Yet Jewish and Arab voters in Israel, and in the city of Acre where they live together, have not allowed extreme nationalists to gain control over the reins of government. Labor has a modest mandate to bring peace to the land within its region.

Spurred on by a major energy crisis the nations of the world are pressing for resolution of the Middle East crisis. Egypt appears to be amenable to negotiations that will permit reopening the Suez Canal. Syria and Israel must find more definitive security arrangements for the Golan Heights. The future of Jerusalem and the fate of the Palestinians challenge the skills of diplomats and persons of good will.

Israel's Jews seem to realize that future wars are unlikely to bring acceptance among Arab neighbors. Local Arab youths have found inspiration in the activities of Palestinian guerrillas. The paths toward reconciliation are drawn out as they have been down through the long history of Acre and its region. The present generation faces dilemmas of choice while the world realizes its stake in the outcome.

Introduction: perceptions of site and situation

> For if a ten years' war made Troy celebrated; if the triumph of the Christian made Antioch more illustrious, Acre will certainly obtain eternal fame as a city for which the whole world contends.
> —Itinerary of King Richard the Lion-hearted

The city of Acre, Israel, is situated at the juncture of two regions, the Mediterranean and the Middle East. This location accounts for the area's attraction to diverse peoples and their cultures, and has also made it vulnerable to repeated conquest. Acre was a port city of the Canaanites some 4000 years ago. For 2000 years, it served variously as a commercial, administrative, and military center under Phoenicians, Egyptians, Assyrians, Persians, Greeks, and Romans. Hebrew tribes came down from the hills to the Plain of Acre, but they had only limited success in occupying the coastal area.

The residents of Acre usually assimilated to the beliefs and customs of imperial conquerors. Over the centuries they embraced Hellenism, Christianity, and Islam, in turn. The Crusades provided an interlude to Muslim Arab dominance for two centuries, until 1291 A.D. when the city was devastated. In the early modern era, Turkish masters of Acre permitted a few European commercial and welfare outposts. There was a renascence of the city under local rulers during the nineteenth-century. Acre was adversely affected by the corruption of the Turkish Empire, and eventually it lost its shipping to a modern port created by the British at Haifa. The Turks lost the area during World War I and the British were granted a Mandate for Palestine through the League of Nations. (The French were similarly compensated in Syria and Lebanon.)

The city of Acre was affected by the conflict that arose in Palestine between Arab and Jewish nationalism. The Arabs sought independence from colonial rule, but they were incensed by the claims of Zionism, which aimed to establish a Jewish homeland in Palestine. The British and the Jews helped to develop Haifa as a transportation and industrial center. Acre became a satellite city that provided labor for the Haifa petroleum refinery and continued to service the Arab villages of the Western Galilee district. The city also gained a reputation as a focal point for Arab resistance to further Jewish expansion in the region. The British maintained a central prison in Acre's old Turkish citadel, and here they detained and sometimes hanged nationalists from both Arab and Jewish insurrectionist groups. Acre prospered during World War II because the Haifa Bay area became a

The walls of Acre as viewed from the beach.

major supply base for the Allied Middle East Command. At war's end, violence erupted and threatened the continuation of British control over Palestine. Arab claims followed the pattern of emerging anticolonial "Third World" movements in Asia, Africa, and elsewhere. The Jews called on the conscience of the world to give them a refuge from the death camps to which the Nazis had condemned them in Europe.

The fortunes of Acre and its people changed drastically as conflicting Arab and Jewish nationalism erupted into war. The United Nations voted a Partition of Palestine into Arab and Jewish states in November 1947. The Jews proclaimed the State of Israel in May 1948. As the British withdrew, armies from neighboring Arab countries invaded. The Arab population fled from the war zones and, for decades, remained as refugees where they crossed the borders of nearby Lebanon, Jordan, or Syria. Of Acre's prewar population of 15,000 Muslim and Christian Arabs, only 1000 stayed. They sought refuge behind the walls of the Old City, where they were joined by a few thousand villagers and marshland nomads who were also in search of safety. The abandoned Arab houses and property were appropriated by Israeli government agencies which were designated as custodians until a permanent peace settlement with the Arab states was reached. In the meantime, the city and its housing were put to use in implementing the government policy of absorbing tens of thousands of Jewish immigrants from Europe, Asia, and Africa who were landing at Haifa port.

The Israeli government planned Acre as a development town of 50,000. Its chief function was to assure Jewish dominance in the Haifa Bay area and the Western Galilee which hitherto had been Arab. The city of Acre was also designated to become a mixed Arab and Jewish center to demonstrate appropriate ways of interaction between the new Jewish majority and the Arab minority. During the first two decades, the Arab population of Acre doubled from 4000 to over 8000, mainly through continued immigration from rural areas and a very high birthrate. Improved government-sponsored health and social services caused a dramatic drop in the Arab deathrate and economic progress was steady. Most Arabs resided in the Old City, on a crowded peninsula of 40 acres surrounded by Turkish period fortifications. But young families were attracted to the New City, where they purchased and rehabilitated eastern-style housing that had been occupied by the Jews during the early postwar period of scarcity. Jewish immigration to Acre from diverse continents mounted steadily to total more than 26,000 during the first two decades. Government agencies directed Jews to Acre to take advantage of its economic potential in the Haifa Bay area and also to keep a high Jewish population ratio relative to the Arabs. Jews filled abandoned Arab houses in the Old as well as the Mandate New Cities. The overflow encamped in tents and huts until new apartment buildings were constructed to form residential quarters to the north and the east of the prewar settlement.

The planned development of Acre was almost entirely dependent on national rather than on local direction and funding. Housing, educational, religious, and social agencies carried out their programs as local bureaus of national ministries. Commercial and industrial site selection and encouragement reflected government and outside private interests, with national concerns dominant. The General Labor Federation (Histadrut) was an overwhelming political and economic force both nationally and locally. It promoted heavy industry and coordinated crafts and public works. Its health and welfare services were utilized to bolster government efforts at Jewish immigrant absorption and provision for the Arab minority.

The development plans for Acre made use of the vistas of the Mediterranean and historical monuments in the interest of national policy to foster tourism and a cosmopolitan image. Special projects concentrated on the period of the Crusades, Turkish fortifications, and Arab folklore. At the same time, a magnificent beach and night clubs along the sea walls were promoted to attract pleasure-seekers. Jewish nationalism was recognized through a patriotic museum that was created from the former British prison in the old Turkish citadel. Both visitors and the local population were made aware of Acre's link to the Zionist cause, despite the city's reputation as a center for hostility to the Jews.

The goals of Acre's development are represented by its municipal emblem, which uses four symbols to link together events of the past and present. These include an ancient sailing vessel and the sea wall; a modern factory and an apartment house. In the case study of Acre which follows, these and other activities are analyzed from the points of view of the city's residents as they respond to national policies and local programs. The vitality of the city is apparent in the conduct of daily life by its diverse population and their participation in ceremonial events which give meaning and a sense of well-being in this troubled world.

1 / Region and locality: crossroads and mosaic

THE CITY OF ACRE IN REGIONAL CONTEXT

The history of Acre follows that of a port city-state caught in a web of recurring regional conflict and forced to bargain for survival. Such places were able to maintain themselves, or even grow, if the mightier powers around them became convinced that they were useful. They were crushed if they rebelled. Some were allowed to decline as rival cities were favored. Occasionally, port city-states expanded through colonization or alliances, or gained advantage when imperial overlords became weak.

The populations of cities like Acre rose or fell according to fortune. They ranged from a few thousand to many tens of thousands, the lower population being more usual. Individuals, families, and tribes were attracted during periods of prosperity or were brought in by imperial design. They might be forced out or decimated when times were harsh. Opportunities associated with Acre's location involved both the sea and the land. These included fishing, farming, and the keeping of herds. Home industries were based on palm fronds and rushes, olive wood branches, and wool and skins. Local tradesmen serviced the merchants and the military who came from more distant places.

The city's skyline showed harbor facilities and fortifications, and multistoried structures of stone which served as offices and residences. Among the groups to be provided for were rulers and administrators, troops, merchants and craftsmen, and laborers. Shrines and temples were located on sites that were or became sacred. They often changed their specific allegiance or sect, according to the power structure of the times. Apartments, warehouses, inns, and barracks might also change function according to need or whim. The city was honeycombed with cisterns and drains, narrow lanes, and staircases that connected the interiors of buildings and granted them limited access to the outside world. Open space within the perimeter of the fortifications was scarce, but some was provided by courtyards within structures and small squares within neighborhoods. Groups of buildings and neighborhood quarters were arranged to serve as defense clusters in times of trouble.

Activity between the walled city and its outside environment was controlled through massive gates built into the fortifications. In times of peace the wealthy and the poor lived on the plain in detached housing of stone or of reeds and palms

View of Acre's Old City from the rooftops.

and sun-baked brick, the quality varied according to station and concern with security. Workers and craftsmen commuted to their sources of supply or employment down by the sea, to the marshlands, or to the plain and the hills. The military used the beach for drill and they manned the walls overlooking the harbor and the plain. The shore also served as a raceway and for promenades. Paths and roads linked the port and villages in the hills and beyond. Farmers traveled with donkeys and merchants used camel caravans with security escorts.

ANCIENT AND CLASSICAL PERIODS

The exact location of Acre's original settlement has not been clearly established. One possible site is the harbor area near which is a mound, called a *tel*. This *Tel el-Fukh-khar* (Mound of the Potsherds) shows later archaeological finds associated with the times of Richard the Lion-hearted and Napoleon, both of whom battled in the area. Other authorities believe the original settlement was at the estuary of the Naaman River, which empties below the harbor site. The ancient Greeks named the stream Belus after the Canaanite deities, the *baalim*. They called the city Aki (cure) after the legendary story of Hercules, who tended his wounds with herbs gathered nearby.

Written records, dating from the Bronze Age before the thirteenth-century B.C., established Ake as a city-state of the Canaanites who occupied much of Palestine at this time. The city's trading potential was developed by the sea-going Phoenicians, who eventually occupied the Levantine coast and sailed the length of the Mediterranean and beyond. Syrian grain was the chief item in trade. This was brought by caravan from inland provinces down a coastal road for regional use and shipment abroad. Tyre and Sidon were better developed ports north of Acre. They were often more successful competitors and they sometimes gained political power over the region. Acre benefited when these neighbors were punished by other more militarily successful imperial states.

As the Iron Age advanced, the coastal and inland cities of Palestine were caught in the squeeze between Egypt to the south and Assyria to the north. The subjection and punishment of the city of 'Akka is included in Egyptian campaign records discovered at Tel el-Amarna. Accounts by the Assyrians, written in cuneiform, give parallel stories of devastation. Also during this period the Israelites had entered the Land of Canaan from the east. In the Book of Judges (I:31) it is mentioned how the city of 'Akko was assigned to the Tribe of Asher, who failed to capture it from the Canaanite defenders. Eventually King David included the Plain of Acre in his "Land of Israel." Solomon acknowledged Phoenician rights in the ports, and he established friendly relations with local rulers in order to obtain supplies for the temple he was building in Jerusalem. Both the Phoenicians and the Hebrews ultimately came under the harsh rule of Babylonia in Mesopotamia. But they gained respite and made progress when the Persians came to power. In the ports Greek commercial interests expanded and anticipated the climactic struggle that ensued between the Persian-dominated lands of the Middle East and the Hellenic states of the eastern Mediterranean.

Acre and its district came under the influence of Hellenistic culture after Alexander the Great defeated the Persians in 333 B.C. After the death of Alexander, his successors based in Egypt and Syria struggled over the lands of the Phoenicians and the Jews. Coinage issued by overlords from the Ptolemies of Egypt indicates that the port of Acre had its name changed to Ptolemais. This name was kept even after Syrian conquest, and it survived through later Hellenistic and Roman periods, as evidenced by records of the Apostle Paul in the Book of Acts (21:7) and the Roman Jewish historian Josephus. The inhabitants of Acre-Ptolemais were assimilated Hellenists, and they were hostile to periodic Jewish nationalist revolts such as those of the Maccabbees against the Syrians.

The city prospered as a base for commerce and security, especially after the stability that came with Roman occupation at the close of the first century B.C. The Roman generals, Pompey and Julius Caesar, early recognized the potential of Acre-Ptolemais as a military base for the penetration of interior provinces. Its commerce continued to prosper through the grain trade from Damascus. Under the Roman Empire a rival port was created at Caesaria, but Acre-Ptolemais continued to serve both commercial and military functions for northern provinces. It played an important role in crushing Jewish revolts in the Galilee. Gradually the city turned from Hellenistic and Jewish concerns toward Christianity as that religion made progress in the Roman Empire.

In the fourth century of the Roman Empire Christianity became officially recognized, and Acre-Ptolemais was assigned to Tyre in the bishopric of Phoenicia. Its civil government was also linked to the coast of the Levant. The city was responsible for taxation and security among the village communities in the district, while its economy was based on landed estates of leading citizens. The city became linked to the fortunes of the Eastern Roman Empire whose center was in Constantinople. As political corruption and economic decay set in, the population was little prepared to meet a new threat from the followers of Muhammed. The Muslims swept out of the Arabian peninsula to gain victory over the Eastern Roman Empire in 636 A.D.

UNDER CALIPHATES AND CRUSADERS

Acre and its region came under the cultural and institutional influence of Arabic Islam beginning with the seventh century A.D., and lasting for 400 hundred years. Its Semitic name was restored and its port became known for its military usefulness and for a ship-building industry which was encouraged by the government. New settlers were brought to the coast from Syria and even Persia. The Caliphate, as the Muslim Arab dominion was called, centered at Damascus during the first century after conquest, and the laws of the Koran and the Arabic language assumed a sacred significance that permeated the region. The basis for unity was *al-umma*, or the Community of Believers. Christians and Jews were tolerated, but they paid a special head-tax and so readily assimilated or converted to the dynamic religious culture of their overlords. Political and religious organization was highly personalized and had limited structure so that factionalism was encouraged. The Caliphate was reestablished in Baghdad, which was remote from the Mediterranean coast. Arab leadership in the provinces was challenged by Turkish factions. Christian power revived under the remnants of the Eastern Roman Empire and gained strength from Italian commercial cities and feudal states in Europe. The city of Acre underwent many sieges and conquests during this period before it came into its greatest glory under the Crusades.

The Crusades were organized during the eleventh century by ambitious European princes, urged on by priests, and supported by the public. They sought to reestablish the Christian claim to Jerusalem and the Holy Land and to gain other advantages as well. They were encouraged by disunity among the Muslim Arabs in the area. The Frankish adventurer, Baldwin I, captured Acre in 1104 with the help of a Genoese fleet. The city was made the chief port in his Latin Kingdom with its capital at Jerusalem. Acre became a supply base with concessions to merchants from the great trading cities of Italy and the French Provence. Its limits expanded beyond the small peninsula up the coast as it enjoyed renewed prosperity. The name of the city was Christianized in memory of Saint John, who was a patron of one of the participating knightly orders. This marked a transition from Hellenistic Ptolemais and Semitic 'Akka to the present European designation, Acre.

Contemporary accounts of the Crusader city of Acre note its division into self-contained quarters. The Genoese were prominent, but they also had to share the limited terrain with their rivals from Pisa, Venice, Amalfi, and Marseilles. Each community had its own piazza or square surrounded by a courthouse and a parish church and storehouses. Each quarter had its mills, bakeries, and butcheries. The city's administration involved a council composed of lay and religious representatives of the sponsoring European states. The Hospitalers of Saint Jean d'Acre nourished the pilgrims who landed at Acre port on the way to Jerusalem. The Templars provided escort based in a castle on the seacoast tip of the peninsula. During periods of truce even Jews and Muslims resided here and visited for pilgrimages. The city's wealth and cosmopolitan nature were noted by the famous Jewish religious philosopher and physician, Maimonides, who came from North Africa in 1165 and by the Spanish Muslim, Ibn Jubair, in 1185.

The fate of Crusader Acre was eventually linked to the contest between the Seljuq Turk, Saladdin, and his Christian opponents. Saladdin overcame the divided Arabic regimes, united Syria and Iraq, and extended his power to Egypt. He crushed the Crusaders decisively at Hittin in 1187, and Acre fell soon after. Saladdin controlled the port until 1191, when the Third Crusade was launched to liberate the Terra Sancta (Holy Land) and Jerusalem again. Philip of France and Richard of England brought up enormous siege machinery and used Greek fire to make Acre Christian once more. However, attempts to retake Jerusalem failed, thus the resources of the Latin Kingdom became concentrated in Acre. The city prospered from the influx of wealth and powerful personages. During truce periods its port was a center for exchange between the lands of the West and the East. The bicultural nature of the city can be seen from its coins, bearing both Arabic and (Latin) Christian inscriptions, which have been discovered as far away as France and Russia. Still, political life in the Crusader domains was rent by internecine conflicts within and among the diverse commercial, religious, and national interests crowded together in the stronghold of Acre. This, together with similar rivalries back in Europe, crippled the ability of the Latin Kingdom to withstand new military pressures imposed by Mongol invaders from Central Asia and the Mamluks, a former slave group that replaced Seljuq Turkish rule in Egypt.

The collapse of Crusader Acre came in 1291 after a long and bloody siege by the Mamluks. The defenders and their families were trapped in their fortifications. The port, citadels, churches, and most other structures were reduced to rubble. The conquerors wished to prevent any future European invasion of the Holy Land. They transferred district administration to Safed in the Galilee. When they eventually permitted visitors and pilgrims to visit the Holy Land and the Galilee, the point of entry was Jaffa port. The lost glory of Acre and the Crusader kingdom heralded the close of an era and the transition from medieval to early modern institutions, such as the nation-state in Europe and eventually in the Middle East.

THE TURKISH PERIOD

After two centuries of reactionary Mamluk rule, the Ottoman Turks captured Syria and Palestine in 1516. The policy of the Sultan Selim and his son, Suleiman the Magnificent, was to restore the Levantine coastal towns and villages in order to encourage trade and to increase security. Foreigners were welcomed for their talents. Jewish refugees from the Spanish Inquisition settled in the Galilee. French merchants were permitted to establish a compound in Acre, which was called the Khan el Afranj. These activities signaled the beginnings of European lay and religious colonization in the lands of the Turkish Empire. Western forms of education and cultural expression, as well as commerce, gained limited entry through treaty privileges, called "Capitulations." European powers advanced their political and military influence in the Middle East through alliances and through direct confrontation with the increasingly corrupt Sultanate in Constantinople and its farflung provincial officials.

By the middle of the eighteenth century, an Arab sheikh from the Galilee, Daher el 'Omar, challenged the central Turkish government and established command in Acre. He ordered the use of Crusader building blocks and other effects for the construction of public and private landmarks. Acre's inner walls, a mosque, and the grain market were monuments to Daher. Christians were permitted to settle to stimulate trade and manufacture. Cotton was imported from the interior and the manufacture of cotton yarn was converted into a monopoly for Daher.

The ascendancy of Acre under Daher was not complete, however. Previous rebels had blocked the harbor to keep out Turkish warships. Daher created an alternative defense system at Haifa, a small walled town at the southern end of Acre Bay, with deep anchorage that could be controlled against invasion from a castle which Daher built above the port. This presaged the ultimate fate of Acre as a bastion and a commercial center.

The Turkish central government reasserted its control over the Levant through the leadership of an Albanian adventurer named Ahmed el Jazzar, nicknamed "the Butcher" for his cruelties. Daher and his family were slain in 1775. Jazzar chose Acre over Sidon for his residence because he favored the site where he had once been held prisoner. His rule extended from Beirut down to Caesaria along the coast and inland toward Damascus. With his increasing wealth he enhanced the fortifications of Acre with elaborate walls and moats. He built a sumptuous palace with magnificent gardens. The town gate was connected to the outside by a drawbridge. Country people were given their own bazaar, and a new main street was lined with specialty shops. Mosques and public baths were expanded, for the population had reached 40,000. The Greek Orthodox and Franciscan churches and European-style hotels date back to this period. Jazzar's ornate mosque and bathhouse were furnished with marble and mosaics brought by sea from Roman ruins at Caesaria. Water came to the city by aqueduct from El Kabri springs in the hills north and east of Acre. Jazzar became increasingly independent of the Turkish central government and he established a monopoly of the trade in grain and cotton. He even banished the French trading colony at a time when the Turks were distracted by one of their periodic wars with Russia.

Acre once more commanded a place on the stage of world history in 1799, when it frustrated Napoleon Bonaparte during the Palestinian invasion that was part of his Egyptian campaign. Jazzar was responsible for local defense, but the grand design involved Turkish troops from the interior provinces and a British fleet commanded by Sir Sidney Smith. The French expeditionary force had taken the coastal cities below Acre and 13,000 men armed with field guns were prepared to destroy this objective if it did not surrender. The French camped on the *tel* overlooking the peninsula and its harbor for 60 days, thus giving it the name Napoleon's Hill, which is still in use today. But the British intercepted the siege artillery which the French had to send by sea. Jazzar's fortifications escaped attempts to blow them up with mines, and he held on until the Turkish army came to his relief from Damascus. By this time Napoleon was receiving adverse reports from his European sources, so he was further inclined to withdraw from the siege and its adjacent districts. Jazzar would have revenged himself on all remaining Christians under his rule, but the British threatened to bomb his capital. During the remaining years, until his death in 1804, Jazzar increased his rapaciousness and cruelty toward all classes of clients and subjects. The treasury of his government was depleted while his personal wealth became legendary. After his death and burial in the courtyard of Jazzar Mosque, an extensive search was made for this trove, but it has never been found.

Jazzar was succeeded by the more gentle-mannered Suleiman Pasha, who was appointed by the Sultanate to rule in Acre. During his 15-year term, he advanced the fortunes of the city and managed it well with the aid of his principal minister, a Jew named Haim Farkhy. They used Crusader stone from the castle at 'Atlit down the coast to restore and add to the defenses. Commercial life was invigorated through the construction of the Suq el Abyad (The White Market). The aqueduct was replaced with a larger one. The Pasha's country house just outside the city had a reputation for its lavishness.

During the rule of 'Abdullah Pasha (1819–1831) improvements in the city continued, but there was political dissension with the central government and new threats from Muhammed 'Ali who had come to power in Egypt. Haim Farkhy was murdered because 'Abdullah Pasha suspected him of conspiring with Constantinople against him. The Egyptian leader made demands on both the Turkish government and the provinces of Syria and the Levant. His son and heir, Ibrahim Bey, besieged Acre in 1831, when it was forced to surrender because the Turks were unable to send relief troops. Europeans were involved in these power struggles to the extent that France supported Egypt since the Egyptian expansion into the Syrian province was in accord with French policy. The British organized a consortium together with the Austrians and Turks and in 1840 put Acre under siege. When a powder magazine between the inner and outer ramparts was hit by sea-borne guns, the explosion resulted in so great a loss of life for the Egyptian defenders that they withdrew permanently and the Turks were restored to control. Though Acre's defenses were repaired and commercial life was reestablished, the conditions of unrest and uncertainty had made their mark. In the latter part of the nineteenth century the city's population declined to 10,000, because it was incapable of coping with the political and economic requirements of the modern world.

The Turkish administration became increasingly dependent on European powers to carry out much of its foreign relations and commercial life. The British preferred to develop Haifa as a port while the French focused on Beirut. Pilgrims disembarked at Jaffa port on the way to Jerusalem, and they visited Acre as part of their tour of the Galilee. The grain trade from Syria declined in international importance as the Americas and other regions increased production by mechanical means. The railroads and steam ships transported grain on a far larger scale than Acre ever provided. Acre became known as a provincial Arab town and was so recorded in 1902 by the political Zionist visionary, Theodore Herzl. In his novel, *Old-New Land*, he depicted a grand Jewish city on Mount Carmel overlooking the bay and the Arab city of Acre on the opposite side. This vision became a reality after World War I, when General Allenby took Palestine for the British in 1918 and the League of Nations authorized a British Mandate. Meanwhile, in November 1917 the British government had issued the Balfour Declaration committing itself to facilitating a Homeland for the Jews in Palestine.

ACRE UNDER THE BRITISH MANDATE FOR PALESTINE

The city of Acre played a passive role in the international events and decisions that followed World War I and the replacement of Turkish rule with the British Mandate for Palestine. Acre's traditional contacts with the Levant were somewhat reduced after the French acquired a Mandate over Syria and Lebanon. In commerce and political affairs, Haifa and Jerusalem became more important to Acre than Beirut and Damascus. The growth of the Haifa Bay area provided work in the port, the railroad yards, the petroleum refinery, and assorted machinery, chemical, and food processing industries which developed with British and Jewish capital investments. Haifa became a major supply base for the Allied Middle East Command during World War II, when Egypt was threatened by the German armies and Syria was under Vichy French rule.

The Acre district also thrived on the growth of agricultural production and the supply of labor to the Haifa Bay area. The city's administrative and commercial functions benefited from the growth of the villages. The Arab population expanded greatly as infant mortality was reduced under the influence of Mandate and Zionist health services. Arab literacy improved with the growth of government and missionary schools at varying levels. Arab pride developed through the influence of the nationalist movement, and it found response in Acre against the Jews and eventually the British. The small Jewish community that had lived in Acre's Old City for generations under the Turks dwindled and ultimately left entirely by the time of World War II. But Jewish national institutions advanced around the Haifa Bay area and up the seacoast beyond Acre. Jewish suburban settlement expanded beyond the Haifa concentration on Mount Carmel. Naharya was founded by German Jews as a seaside town midway between Acre and the Lebanese border. Agricultural communes and villages were founded by the Zionists on reclaimed marshlands below and beyond the walls of Acre.

The British authorities tried to cope with conflicting Arab and Jewish nationalism in the area by increasing their security forces. They converted the old Turkish citadel into the central prison for Palestine. They constructed a police barracks, called a Taggart fortress, along the seacoast in the New City. Finally, they quartered army units on the northern perimeters of potential residential expansion, hoping thereby to suppress threats to the peace and to maintain their control. In their attempts to appear even-handed, the British Mandate officials earned the resentment of nationalist leaders on both sides and eventually that of the population, which was drawn to nationalist causes.

Modernization came slowly to Acre during the period of the British Mandate. Old structures and institutions sometimes found new uses. For example, the camel caravan stops were converted into truck repair stations, metal workshops, and processing plants for tobacco and olive oil. Almost no trading vessels called at the port, but fishing continued and found a ready market in the district and among tourists. The mosques and churches remained centers for religious and communal life. The British continued the tradition of assigning family affairs to the jurisdiction of religious courts. The walls of Acre were breached in two places to permit motor roads between the Old City and the New City, which was expanding due to the growth of population and the effect of prosperity. From a 1922 official census record low of 6420 residents, the population had risen to more than 15,000 during the period of World War II.

British Mandate officials sought to help the city expand and to introduce modern planning and development methods. In 1945, oblivious to the portents of nationalist struggle, Senior Architect Percy H. Winter issued a basic survey report for the Public Works Department of the Government of Palestine. He urged reconstruction to relieve the crowded situation in Acre's Old City. He feared that the city's population would increase by another 50 percent within 20 years because of the continued high birthrate and emigration from the villages. His survey of Acre's Old City counted 8500 residents with an average of 3.2 persons per room. Household size averaged six or more persons, with several generations living under one roof. There was almost no town sewage, garbage disposal, or street repair service. Interviews with young couples showed that they were desirous of moving outside the walled city to their own homes or apartments. The Winter report called for revisions in the Mandate Housing Act of 1919 which had failed to change the conditions of residential housing and attendant problems.

The 1945 report recommended major land-use and development proposals, such as the following: the government should apply pressure on landlords to maintain and develop their property; state lands inherited from the Turkish regime could be used as a source for new settlement; some agricultural lands would have to be rezoned for residential or other uses, with the exception of the government stock farm, which remained as a reserve for emergency periods. The Bahai religious group, whose extensive holdings dated from the nineteenth century when they found refuge from persecution in Persia, must be persuaded to relinquish the land for contemporary uses; swampland south of the city should be reclaimed to provide public works and sites for oil storage and light industry; the old Turkish railroad could be realigned to permit expansion of public gardens in the New City; the unspoiled beaches could be developed for recreation, with yachting in the bay and a promenade among the palm groves along the shore. Within the Old City, the report urged the revival of fishing by organizing the fishermen into a guild and promoting boat building and repair. It called for expansion of the market into the Khan es Shawarda, adding shops for carpentry and metal work and storehouses.

A most exciting part of the Winter report for the development of Acre was its plan for the drainage of the Top Alti Swamp north of the settled area and for its transformation into a modern center for the expanded city. The Municipality and a mosque, a market, and a transportation terminal for commuters and visitors would be relocated here. This would cover some eight acres or more, which now provided storm water runoff during the winter rainy season. Further to the north was the 50 acre Manshiyah Swamp. This would be reclaimed at first for agriculture and then for settlement. The details of commercial and industrial zoning and development rounded out this highly competent and prophetic document.

The Winter report was a rational plan for the transformation of residential, commercial, and industrial centers from a traditional and limited Old City to a modernized New City of Acre. This plan has in effect been the basis for the growth of contemporary Acre. But the sponsors were neither the British Mandate nor the Arab residents. Rather, the development of Acre became public and national policy of the Jews, who came into control during the 1948 Arab-Israeli war. In the effort to relocate thousands of Jewish immigrants, the new authorities drained the swamps and established zones for industry and for new civic, religious, and commercial centers beyond the walls of Acre.

2 / A development city in Israel

THE ARAB-ISRAELI WAR AND ITS AFTERMATH

By the end of the 1930s and through World War II, nationalistic tensions in Palestine mounted, making the British Mandate there untenable. In response to Arab protests and accelerated violence, the British had sent numerous investigating commissions to assess the absorptive capacity of the country for immigration and the wishes of its inhabitants concerning independent territories. In 1939, on the eve of World War II, the British halted further Jewish immigration into Palestine and left the Jews to their fate in Europe. Zionist leaders made the reluctant decision to cooperate with the government in fighting the very real threat of German invasion in the Middle East. They resorted to clandestine and often disasterous attempts to rescue their brethren and they sharpened their military skills.

At the end of World War II, the western world felt compassion and perhaps guilt for the holocaust causing the death of six million Jews among other victims of the Nazis in Europe. They showed little sympathy for the British position in Palestine. Also, some countries viewed this as an opportunity to gain influence with nationalistic groups that sought to oust the colonial regime. The crisis was sharpened by the news of foundering refugee ships, imprisonment of the rescuers, Jewish terrorist and British counter-terrorist actions, and mounting Arab criticism of a possible western sell-out to the Zionists. In 1947 there was a massive escape by Jewish nationalist prisoners from Acre prison. In Arab villages and cities nationalist leaders with foreign support and direction intimidated and punished collaborators and neutrals. The British finally declared the Mandate unworkable and turned over the future of Palestine to the United Nations. Major cities and centers of Jewish rural colonization were allotted to a Jewish state. The Arabs were assigned Acre and the Galilee and the hills of the Jordan River west bank. Nobody was satisfied and they prepared for military confrontation after the British withdrew.

As Arab armies from neighboring countries poured over the borders, the Zionist leaders declared the State of Israel in May 1948. The Proclamation of Independence of the Jewish state gave primary attention to The Ingathering of the Exiles, or the absorption of Jewish immigrants. It also promised the Arabs under its jurisdiction full civil rights as a minority. Arabs were requested to remain in their communities and to participate as citizens in the development of the state.

But the Arab High Command, which represented nationalist leaders drawn from Palestine and its neighboring countries, exhorted the Arab masses to flee the area of fighting. They promised to drive the Jews into the sea and to reward the Arab people with independence and booty. Jewish atrocities in certain Arab villages further agitated these confused people. Most of the residents of Haifa and Acre fled to the nearest borders of Lebanon, Syria, and Arab Palestine, which was occupied by Jordan. Villages and cities were deserted, not temporarily as originally thought, but for decades while people lived in refugee camps in unfriendly lands. Only a remnant of the Arab residents of Jewish occupied Palestine remained to care for family property. Others were too feeble or too dispirited to move. The walls of Acre gave a feeling of refuge and about 1000 native inhabitants sought shelter in mosques and churches during the fighting, as was the age-old custom. It was sensed that the enemy would respect religious structures more than any other, and they did.

On May 16, 1948, the Golani Brigade of the Israeli Defense Forces confronted a small Arab garrison at the police barracks at Acre. The veterans of the Haganah, the more moderate and widely supported Jewish military group, had come up the road from Haifa and from agricultural settlements around the walled city. Fighting was sporadic for a day or two until the Arab civilian leaders sent a priest to Tel Napoleon to hoist the white flag of surrender and to undertake negotiations. This brought the once-proud Arab nationalist center of Acre and the Western Galilee under Jewish control and opened it to Jewish settlement. Order was restored in the city through military government and a civilian council of local Arab notables. The United Nations supervised relief for Arab refugees, which now included villagers and nomads who had sought shelter in the walled city. In the meantime, Israeli government ministries made comprehensive plans for the relocation of thousands of Jewish immigrants who were landing at Haifa port. The city of Acre, with much of its housing abandoned and its location strategic to Haifa and the Galilee, was to play an important role in further governmental development plans. It readily suited the model for a development city in Israel by fulfilling government policies for Jewish immigrant absorption. There was sufficient land in the north and east for residential construction. Commuting distance to Haifa and the Bay area was reasonable for workers. Government agencies directed industrial planners and investors here and sites were made available. The government decided to make Acre politically autonomous from Haifa in order to develop its character and to promote a network of services within the district.

The mixed Arab-Jewish presence in Acre provided an opportunity to experiment with intergroup relations at the municipal and district level as well as the good public relations needed by the state of Israel. Furthermore, Arab enterprise and the relics of Acre's Old City attracted tourists who came from many lands and who were interested in the Crusader period and Middle Eastern lore. At this time, Acre provided the best vista of Arab city life in Israel, with the exception of Nazareth in the Galilee.

The development of Acre and the Western Galilee also served the security needs of the state of Israel. Young Israeli war veterans and vigorous immigrants were among the first settlers directed to the city and its district. Housing was made available to young couples and public assistance was given to children and to older parents who, for reasons of traditional family custom, might be required to live with the veterans. The military atmosphere of Acre was much in evidence. Paramilitary police provided for internal security in the region. They were quartered in the Taggart fortress on the seacoast of the New City. The streets of Acre attracted young men and women troops who were spending their leave at a furlough base located near the expansive beach. There was a large army training base located beyond the northern limits of Acre. A nautical college was founded and placed between the beach and the old Turkish fortifications. Some Druzes and Arabs served on border police patrols, but the main force of security and its planning was in the hands of the Jews.

THE FIRST STAGES OF DEVELOPMENT

Many public and private agencies were involved in implementing the government's plan to develop the city of Acre as a district center with a population of 50,000. A military governor was appointed by the Ministry of Defense to cope with the immediate postwar confusion and to reduce the tensions. The Ministry of the Interior became responsible for organizing the municipal government and for arranging elections as soon as feasible. The Jewish Agency, which represented the World Zionist Organization, sponsored the transportation of immigrants and provided for their needs during the first year of their settlement in Israel. Government ministries collaborated with the Jewish Agency to extend programs that would encourage absorption. These included housing, employment, education, and related social and cultural services. The General Federation of Jewish Labor, through its Haifa Workers' Council, helped to establish a local branch of Histadrut, the Labor Federation, in Acre. The government encouraged these activities, which included the negotiation and supervision of employment contracts, vocational training, and assorted health and welfare services for workers and their families. Eventually, similar services were developed for the Arab minority, with specially integrated sections staffed by Arabs. Philanthropic health and welfare projects affiliated with religious, labor, and general Zionist movements were also in evidence. The many political parties in Israel became involved in individual and group services and recruitment.

The development administrators were concerned with the allocation of property and housing, especially for the refugees and immigrants. The government created Amidar, the Housing Development Corporation, to rent and rehabilitate, and eventually to construct housing for Jews and for Arabs. Property vacated by Arab refugees was turned over to the Custodian for Abandoned Property for redistribution pending final settlement with the original owners. Even residents who had sought temporary refuge outside their homes during the war faced frustrating delays in regaining the use of their property and its income. The dislocations and the lack of confidence in Israel's authority and financial prospects caused great bitterness among Arabs everywhere and led to extreme political denunciations.

For national security reasons and for long-range planning purposes, Acre's Old

In the suq—Old City marketplace.

City was designated for Arab occupancy while new quarters were constructed beyond the Mandate New City for the Jews. In the early postwar years, Jews were directed to housing in the Old City, but gradually they were relocated to the new neighborhoods. Arabs only began to return to former homes or to newly purchased residences in the Mandate New City as Jews transferred to more modern apartments in Acre. Many of the veteran Jewish settlers moved to suburbs such as Naharya or the Haifa Bay area. Many single houses in the Mandate New City were taken by the government and the sites were converted into apartments which generally attracted Jews, though some Arabs were willing to try an integrated style of living. Official rents were nominal but real costs were high because the scarcity of housing led to free market transactions, such as the giving of "key money" by tenants as apartments changed hands. Housing quality improved as institutional and private investments sponsored new projects. Fully employed residents moved to these new apartments and the poor were subsidized and relocated from substandard units, especially from the Old City.

Both Arabs and Jews faced common problems of austerity during the early postwar and development years of Israel. The government controlled the production and distribution and prices of food, clothing, and most other necessities in order to cope with the population influx and the lack of capital resources. In the local markets, such as the *suq* in Acre's Old City, Jewish immigrants and Arab natives intermingled and bartered their possessions. Basic foods such as bread, dairy products, fish, fruits, and vegetables were generally available at nominal cost. Meat, cooking oil, rice, and imported items such as tea, coffee, and sugar were more scarce and became products of black market. Residents limited their purchases or resorted to the free market according to the pressures of hospitality and custom as much as to the possession of wealth. In general, most citizens felt themselves to be equally deprived, but they hoped for better times.

There was considerable underemployment and a reliance on public works and welfare services during the austerity period. Local authorities pressured their national counterparts for greater commitments to local industrial development and subsidies for workshops and cooperative enterprises. The government favored those projects that could earn foreign currency over those that merely satisfied a demand for consumer goods. The government was able to attract overseas Jewish philanthropic investment to the Haifa Bay area and this was supplemented by reparations payments by West Germany and venture capital from Israel's labor movement and private sources. The industries that developed included a steel

Arab–Jewish exchange in the marketplace.

processing plant, which used scrap metals, and factories for chemicals, textiles, and food canning. Outsiders provided the capital and the administrative expertise, but the workers were recruited from among the immigrants through labor unions and labor exchanges. However, several years passed until such industry began to operate, so that the lives of the immigrants were dominated by public works projects involving clearing rubble, draining swamps, and planting trees. Construction work paid more attractive wages and had the benefits of strong labor union involvement. But the physical demands were hard on Jewish immigrants drawn from urban crafts, trades, or clerical backgrounds, though many did change their calling as they acquired skills in construction. Rural Arabs were most attracted to construction, but it alienated those educated to expect bureaucratic employment. Jews with overseas education became qualified for bureaucratic and professional posts when they completed Hebrew language and special skills courses. Political parties recruited members on the basis of their ability to provide work and advancement. Both Jews and Arabs became involved in labor movement activity, or else they supported opposition and sometimes extremist parties when they could gain more in this way.

The government consciously planned educational and related programs for the youth of the country. Schooling for Arabs and Jews was compulsory and free through the eighth grade. In addition, both nursery schools and secondary schools were encouraged and partially subsidized. For Jewish children, the government objective was to fuse the diverse ethnic groups that had come from traditional and modern, eastern and western cultures. The curriculum emphasized the Hebrew language and Jewish and Zionist historical and philosophical subjects. Technical skills were developed later at more specialized levels. Youth movements were encouraged by the political parties, except for the Scouts, which was considered to be nonpolitical. Jewish youth was subjected to orientations that ranged from religious and nationalist to socialist, but all movements promoted forms of Jewish identity and a love for Israel as the Jewish Homeland.

Educational programs and services for Arab children and youth were designed to incorporate Muslim or Christian religious traditions and history, while playing down extreme nationalist ideology. Cultural autonomy and pride in Arab peoplehood were emphasized in Arab language training, within a pragmatic context of life in Israel as a modern, democratic, welfare-oriented state. Jewish administrators were used until Arab teachers and administrators could be recruited and trained, since most intellectuals had fled during the war. This caused great resentment among the Arabs and put unpleasant pressure on those Iraqi, Syrian, or Egyptian Jews who found themselves in such positions. In due course, texts produced locally plus new staff personnel made the government schools more significant in the Arab community. Technical training programs were most widely accepted, and there was pressure for Hebrew language skills as well.

Most of Acre's Christian Arab population, as well as Muslim Arabs of status, sent their children to Terra Sancta parochial school, which was operated by the Franciscans in the Khan el Afranj compound. Arab nationalists found the parochial schools to be a useful link with overseas western countries and a check on Jewish nationalist domination. Leadership in the American Friends Service Committee community center also came from among these Arab families. There was a class and status separation between these and Muslim Arab refugees from the villages and nomadic groups, who tended to become absorbed in Acre's working-class culture. Middle-class Arabs grew dissatisfied as Jews replaced them in bureaucratic and highly skilled occupations. Many planned to emigrate through their overseas contacts, while others joined extremist political movements.

Political affairs dominate the relations between the city of Acre and the state of Israel. During the early period of development they were worked out through the establishment of the Municipality. The military government lasted for one year and preparations were made for local elections according to laws supervised by the Ministry of the Interior. Franchise to vote included men and women from the age of 18, who could prove they resided in the city. There was no test of literacy or property, which many immigrants and refugees had been accustomed to under other regimes. Under military government there had been a provisional council of five members, which included three Jews and two Arabs. Government ministry representatives also played an adjunct role in council deliberations because of the preliminary nature of the city's structure and its state of development.

The first municipal council under civilian control was to comprise twelve members, according to a special formula related to population and circumstances of development. There would be three Arab and three Jewish residents and six representatives from government ministries. Political control was assured to Labor and Religious parties, who were identified with the national leadership under David Ben-Gurion or else with Jewish tradition, which appealed both to western and eastern immigrants. Opposition parties included Marxist Labor and the Communists on the left. They received some votes from anti-Zionist Arabs and from European Jews who felt beholden to the Russians during World War II. Right-wing opposition parties included the General Zionists, who were led by businessmen, and the Herut (Freedom), who were opposed to socialist labor domination and who were identified with Jewish nationalists from the period of struggle against the British and the Arabs. Jews from Arab lands, who did not vote for Labor or for the Religious parties, often supported the Herut movement because of its anti-Arab reputation which, however, became modified over time. These patterns were repeated and reinforced during national and municipal elections in 1951. At that time, the municipal council constituted thirteen members, all of whom were local residents. This was a sign that the government recognized the value of local autonomy, as long as there were strong ties to national political institutions.

The early period of Acre as a development city in Israel showed a significant rise in the population and a transformation of the physical characteristics of this former Arab stronghold. The city, which was abandoned in 1948, reached a population of 12,000 in 1950 as Jewish immigrants were brought to the older sections, at first living among Arab refugees. The overflow of Jews was housed in transient camps spread out over agricultural fields on the outskirts of the built-up city. The government authorized an enlargement of the municipal boundaries to 3000 acres, which made Acre, Israel, larger than either the Crusader city or the city of Jazzar's time. The Ministry of the Interior acquired the lands north and east of the Mandate New City over the objections of the Ministry of Agriculture. The transfer of land from agricultural to urban and industrial use showed the primary importance the government placed on such land-use for massive immigrant absorption.

The new immigrant neighborhoods were characterized by apartment house complexes of concrete block, three or four stories in height, with two or three rooms and balconies. Landscaping and play areas gave some relief to the monotony and attempted to serve the recreational needs of the many children and their elders. In the centers were small food shops and general stores, kindergartens, and occasionally clubhouses and small synagogues. There were branches of banks and government bureaus servicing employment, health, and welfare. There were connecting streets and roads leading to the main shopping center and bureau headquarters in the New City. In general, the further the family lived from Ben Ami Street and its bright lights and promenade, the more isolated it felt from the mainstream of the city's life. Families with large numbers of children and low employment skills began to sense a relative deprivation after the first period of joy in being in the Jewish Homeland. They found some satisfaction when it was possible to provide neighborhood housing and amenities for kinship groups, though the younger generation soon sought independent housing and more space. The political parties became involved in the efforts of residents to improve their situation. They attracted partisans by their ability to help them or at least not to alienate them.

In 1960, at the end of its first dozen years of development, the population of Acre reached 25,000. Industries were operating along the Haifa Bay area. Workshops and small businesses were scattered within the Old City and the Mandate New City. Officials were trying to convince the public and its representatives of the need for concern with waste disposal, noise, and general aesthetic considerations. Publicity in the newspapers reinforced the image of Acre as a somewhat romantic and bustling, but incredibly unkempt place. The city's leaders wished to modernize life, particularly in the New City, to make living here attractive to young couples and the middle class. They approved the removal of small Arab houses and a match factory from the city's main street and replaced these with substantial apartments and retail shops. The public gardens were extended through low-lying areas, called *wadis*, which once provided defenses for the Old City. The public works employees tended their flowering shrubs with great devotion, and family groups and couples enjoyed the pleasant surroundings, especially on the Sabbath and holidays.

The planners continued to separate residential neighborhoods from business and industrial zones, following the Mandate government's approach. This was a reaction against the hodge-podge of the preindustrial city, but it was not always the most feasible arrangement for the widely dispersed immigrant settlers who were forced to commute for most of their daily needs. Internal bus transportation was introduced, but large numbers continued to walk long distances and youths bicycled. Motor vehicle ownership increased among some middle-class families, but among the younger workers motor bikes were more popular. Buses and group taxis gave fairly reliable service to the Haifa Bay area and the Galilee, but plans for a large central transportation terminal and shopping complex in the city's new center were still unrealized by the early 1970s. Beyond these frustrations, however, the visitor to Acre gained an impression of vitality and a population mix. Ethnic groups in distinctive clothing comingled with workers and clerks on the streets and in the service bureaus. Urban dwellers, villagers, and tourists were attracted to the stone walls and the sea which provided a proscenium for more recently developed apartments and factories.

THE ROLE OF STRONG LEADERSHIP

For the development of Acre to succeed there was a need for strong leaders who could inspire confidence among the local population as well as among national officials who were in control of resources. The city was in competition with similar immigrant towns in its claims for national attention, but it had certain bargaining advantages because of its mixed Arab-Jewish population. Political action was the link connecting the city and the national power structure. Political parties and their leadership provided the instruments for achieving both public and private objectives. The first two mayors of Acre, Israel, set the directions and the pace for the city's growth. Their tenure ended when unsolvable economic, social, and political problems overwhelmed them. But at each stage there had been achievements and these were recognized together with the failures.

Arab and Jewish children at play in the Old City.

Political affairs dominate much of the daily communications that take place in Acre and in Israel. There are more than a dozen political parties, and these are continuously splintering or else forming coalitions. They range in ideology from traditional and nationalist through socialist, but their success is based on satisfying the basic needs of the electorate rather than party lines. Elections for the National Assembly (called the Knesseth), the Municipality, and the General Federation of Labor occur with regularity approximately every four years.

Political parties gain seats through a system of proportional representation for the municipal, national, and labor union elections. Parties make up lists of candidates and the voters select a single ballot. The number of party choices to gain office depends on the percentage the party receives among all ballots cast. Party leaders usually head the lists. Succeeding candidates are selected according to district, ethnicity, occupation, or other suitable attribute of interest to a diverse electorate. In Acre, it is possible for a Labor party list to consist of a European Jewish lawyer, a North African labor union leader, an Egyptian Jewish engineer, and so forth. The more leftist party, MAPAM, integrates Arabs with Jews on its lists. Candidates move up to take office when vacancies occur among incumbents near the head of the list.

The system allows for great diversity within parties, but there is little direct selection by those who are not party regulars. The party secretary is powerful, as is his executive committee. National parties and their leaders control much of the funding and the policy, especially when coalitions are in order. Local preferences are often disregarded, which leads to personality clashes within municipal coalitions. The parties are expected to provide personal service to potential voters. They recruit active members among those who are ambitious for office or favors. They also change leaders when major dissatisfaction gives rise to dissenting factions.

The political system in Acre and in Israel has generally been stable despite the rise and fall of numerous individual officials and widespread public criticism by oppositon parties. Coalition governments both nationally and locally have been dominated by MAPAI, the Labor party, whose leaders include David Ben-Gurion and Golda Meir. Various Jewish Religious parties have found it advantageous to join the coalitions in order to gain a place for traditional practices in a society that is rapidly secularizing. The Communist party on the left is never in a coalition. Rightist entrepreneurs and nationalists sometimes join a coalition during times of extreme national danger.

Political activity in Acre and in Israel is the nexus between those who have or seek the power to act and those who seek or require their needs to be served. This political activity permeates all ethnic, class, and status groups and crosses party ideologies. Immigrant Jews and refugee Arabs respect power and desire competent authority. They prefer a personal approach rather than a professionalized bureaucracy. The middle classes and the labor bureaucrats try to maintain control among all the parties. The workers have gained political experience through labor councils, strikes, and negotiations. European Jews fear the rise of eastern Jews and both groups are wary of the ability of the Arabs to make headway through coalition. The Arab minority joins those Jewish parties that can help and withholds support from those it feels are hostile or ineffective. Youths learn politics within their families and through their peer group movements. Many are disdainful of the factionalism, but there is a cadre of ambitious young people in each party who strive to serve and thus gain office.

The first mayor of Acre, Israel, was Baruch Noy, a successful military governor who gained the backing of the Labor and Religious coalition. It was felt that he could cope with the problems posed by the austerity and that he would be able to bring about government help for construction of housing and industrial plants. The mayor was zealous in responding to the multitude of personal and group demands during a period of great unemployment, currency inflation, and personal stress among the immigrants and refugees. He appeared to be able to argue forcefully with government officials for Acre to receive its share of aid. But the mayor could not overcome the national dimensions of this survival crisis, nor could he satisfy the personal ambitions of local individuals. Reports were circulated that the mayor had profited from construction contracts and that his administration lacked systems of auditing and other controls. He was challenged within his political party and was investigated by a committee of the Israeli National Assembly. The adverse publicity lost him further support in Acre, especially when the Municipality was placed under the Ministry of the Interior, which acted as caretaker. He resigned in ignominy and eventually went overseas, where he died. There is one memorial in a street named after his son who was killed in the Israeli War of Independence. Otherwise his era is recalled as one of improvisation to cope with survival and subsistence. Opposing political parties and national authorities have used scandals such as this to justify limiting municipal autonomy and control from above and newspaper reporters have readily dredged up this incident, thereby giving the city of Acre an image of immaturity and disorder.

The second mayor of Acre, Joseph Gadish, took office in 1952. He was the leader of the local MAPAI party that unseated its previous incumbent. The new mayor came from a background of Zionist philosophy, experience in a kibbutz and the war, and a career in education administration. He has been called the "Napoleon of 'Akko," for his grand schemes for the city's development and for his ability to wrest funds from and to influence government bureaus. It was during this period that the austerity ended and employment increased with industrial and labor movement expansion. Schools and other institutions serving youth kept pace with the needs of new neighborhoods. Religious groups founded additional synagogues and gained support for institutionalized ritual services, such as marriage bureaus, bathhouses, and slaughterhouses. The mayor paid special attention to the Arab population, studying the Arabic language and customs. He improved his ability to communicate with Jews from eastern countries as well as with the Muslim and Christian communities. Eventually, he used these talents to prepare himself for a major educational post in the minorities division of the Ministry of Education.

Mayor Gadish hosted artists and tourist groups in order to promote the panorama and the relics of Acre for the city's benefit. He negotiated with the Prime Minister's Office and its division which was concerned with the Preservation of Historic Sites and with the Ministry of Tourism to restore the sea wall, the Hospitaler Crypt of Saint John, Jazzar's Mosque and the Hammam (Bathhouse).

An Arabic folklore museum was promoted in the chambers of the bathhouse and to it were added archeological and artistic exhibits for tourism. The movie *Exodus* was filmed here and at the fortress prison, where a nationalist museum had begun. Promenades and cafes were developed to make Acre into a modern beach resort as well as a historical center.

Tendencies in Arab-Jewish intergroup relations during the middle and later 1950s favored integration in political and economic affairs. The Arabs supported the Labor party coalition through their own affiliated groups. Their leaders were appointed as Deputy Mayor and member of the local Histadrut executive committee respectively. The general employment situation was favorable for all groups so that the Arabs could pressure for better conditions in construction work, for training courses, and for positions in the service bureaus. Arab population doubled during this period and younger families were beginning to purchase and to rent housing in the Mandate New City. During the 1956 Sinai campaign by the Israelis against Egypt, Acre's Old City was relatively tranquil.

Resentment by the Arabs was never far from the surface, however, and this affected their relations with the mayor and the Jewish majority. In 1961 some Arab infiltrators were intercepted by patrols on a distant border and shot dead. Rumors spread throughout Arab settlements that the youths had been mutilated. In Acre's Old City streets there were demonstrations by Terra Sancta school pupils. They were led by the wife of the Communist party leader, who was an Arab of Greek Orthodox background. The carefully nurtured years of Arab-Jewish cooperation were shattered when Oriental Jews returning from work broke into the Old City and beat up the youths. The police detained the Arab leaders but did not prosecute the Jews. Though the demonstration appeared to be part of leftist opposition to the popularity of the Labor coalition, it also expressed the latent nationalist feelings of the Arabs. The journalists again accused Acre's municipal government of inability to deal justly with the minority. Ironically, Gadish was invited to Jerusalem soon afterward, where he assumed his position as expert for Arab education.

LIMITATIONS TO GROWTH

The signs of progress of Acre as a development city were evident in the series of dedication ceremonies for new facilities and landmarks during the decades that passed. Yet these were also years of political, labor, and ethnic tension. Jewish immigration continued, but it began to slow down by the late 1960s. There was a national recession in the middle of this decade. After the Six-Day War in 1967, much new settlement was directed to the Jerusalem area and the southern part of the country. Acre and the Galilee demanded attention because of the high Arab birth rate and a deteriorating security situation.

The growth of Acre benefited individuals and groups who were able to improve their material and their social lives. The refugees were ambitious to acquire symbols of success for themselves and their children. They felt deprived of goods and status during the persecutions overseas. Many adult families viewed the city as a refuge and they were pleased with its progress. Others felt the progress benefited groups other than their own. For this reason, many middle-class European Jews were departing for neighboring suburbs. Oriental Jews challenged the dominance of European Jews in the government bureaucracy. Arabs supported the Communist party, which had taken up the thrice-lost nationalist cause. Amidst the progress materialism and careerism seemed to be competing with nationalist and social democratic ideology.

There was a cry for leadership that would overcome the political factionalism and manage the affairs of the city. The mayors who succeeded Gadish had been chosen through political and Labor party compromise. Their tenure was made difficult by the unstable coalitions among ambitious ethnic groups and individuals.

By the time of its third decade, during the early 1970s, the population of Acre was stabilizing at under 40,000. There was new housing, industrial enterprise, tourism, and a feeling of involvement in the nation's prosperity, which was associated with technological innovation and productivity. The malaise in Acre perhaps reflected the quest for an image that was unrealistic. There was a question whether a city of workers in an oriental atmosphere could govern itself and develop institutions that would serve the present and future generations.

Government planners had expected Acre to be satellite to Haifa and the suburban and rural settlements in the Bay area. Its administrators and professionals would find personal satisfaction and gain status from local success and the city's historical and maritime ambience. Acre's Rotary Club symbolized such fellowship among cultivated persons of diverse ethnic backgrounds. But the masses of the population identified with the workingman's culture and its political social welfare orientations. The new generation sought mechanical training and office skills. Those who found satisfaction in work, in family, and in civic life remained, but large numbers left for areas with greater technological or professional potential, including overseas. The city was a way-station for the early settlers of 1948 and for their children. Its management would require mature judgment and tolerance of diversity. Government intervention would continue as long as the international situation, particularly the Arab hostility toward Israel and its policies, remained a daily concern. National and local goals joined and became the framework for personal achievement. Conflict, factionalism, and alienation were signs that these goals and frameworks were imperfectly integrated.

3 / The Arab minority

The presence of the Arabs in Acre gives the city a unique character in Israel. There are approximately 6000 Muslims and more than 2000 Christians combined with a small number of Bahai and Druze. This population is now more then double the remnant of refugees who sought shelter behind the walls of the Old City during the 1948 Arab-Israeli War. Few of these residents are original families; indeed, even those who are native residents cite village and tribal origins for their parents or grandparents. The Christians are predominantly of Mediterranean origin. Many Muslims are Negroid, with their ancestry in the Nile Valley and Haifa Bay area marshlands. Tribal groups and villagers from Jordan and Syria came to the coastal area or else were brought here under Turkish and British Mandate regimes.

The leading Arab elite of Acre come from the few propertied or well-educated families who remained behind during the 1948 Arab-Israeli War. They include successful bureaucrats and workers who have utilized for their advancement the political opportunities of coalition with the Labor party and activity within the Labor Federation. Leadership within the Arab community is sectarian among the Muslim and various Christian groups. It includes nationalists who openly oppose coalition as well as those who seem to have accommodated to the facts of Arab minority life in Israel. There are three or four Arab members in the Acre Municipal Council. One representative who is in the Labor coalition is also designated a Deputy Mayor. There is usually an Arab of the Communist party who leads the opposition. The practicalities of joint or separate Arab-Jewish party lists vary with national political policies and the personalites involved.

Most of Acre's Arabs live in the Old City, by circumstance and by choice, but the younger and more successful Arab families tend to purchase housing in the Mandate New City. Most Arab families have households of six or more persons, with one-fourth of the households containing nine or more persons. The more traditional families have the larger numbers and they also tend to be poorer. But younger couples are following westernized and Jewish preferences for somewhat smaller families and more modern apartment housing. The Arabs have resisted relocation to apartments located in remote Jewish immigrant quarters. The wars and nationalistic tensions have caused the Arabs to prefer the security of living together rather than dispersing among Jewish families or neighborhoods. But there are plans to rehabilitate the Old City for tourism under the Old Acre Development Corporation. This is progressing slowly, from the waterfront area to Crusader sites near the inner walls, and involves some family relocation.

PUBLIC LIFE

Arab life in Acre continues patterns from the early modern period which saw the transition from Turkish to British rule. In this respect, it is similar to urban life in other countries of the Levant. In Acre's Old City there are narrow alleys of cobble stone with rain gutters down their centers. House fronts have exteriors that are anonymous. Interiors are reached through courtyards and up staircases of stone and cement. Unwanted intruders are barred by iron grillwork in the windows. Additional security, combining folk tradition and religion, is sought by painting or affixing to the door posts crosses, crescents, stars, or hands of blue indigo.

Neighborhood quarters are only vaguely defined since the upheaval in 1948. Christian Arabs live near their churches where they own commercial and residential property. The Bahai control institutional and some residential holdings within the Old City, but the Persian Gardens, the estate of the Irani family, and unused tracts are beyond the walls and toward the city limits. Aside from dwellings and shops owned privately, there is considerable property held by the *waqf*, which is the Muslim charitable foundation. Some of the shops near the Jazzar Mosque and the Crypt of Saint John have been rehabilitated and rented out for the tourist trade.

Most of the property of the Arabs of Acre came under the Custodian for Abandoned Property, and most housing is rented through Amidar, the government housing corporation. This permits the refugees to pay low rents and it encourages a policy of family transfer to improved dwellings. The private housing market is beyond the means of most Arab families, but ambitious workers combine their resources to make purchases and to rehabilitate them to taste. A few leading families have moved into modern luxury apartments in the New City near the public gardens. Others have tried an experiment in integrated housing for young couples who are Arab and Jewish.

Relations between neighbors vary with the degree of kinship, ethnicity, and common cultural or institutional interests. Childrens' quarrels are often a source for larger sectarian or communal disputes. Families are aware of this and try to avoid situations that might lead to such strife. Daily interpersonal and intergroup relations tend to be pragmatic and outwardly courteous. Hostilities become public during periodic crises, usually triggered by an external event such as a border incident. Then ethnic and religious identification is most significant in interpersonal and intergroup relations. But traditional patrilineal and patrilocal controls have been upset by the wars and dislocations, and by modernization itself. Young people have formed friendships among schoolmates, labor union groups, political parties, and recreational associates. However, ethnic selectivity may decide in advance who will interact at a school, on the job, in political party life, or at the cafe. The American Friends Service Committee discovered that its community center activities drew upon existing friendship and kin groups. The active participants generated their own civic and cultural group which persisted long after the departure of the Quakers during the early 1960s.

The center of commercial life for Arabs is the *suq*, the traditional market in the Old City. It begins at a square which is fronted by office buildings and a bus terminal and runs like a spine down toward the fishermen's harbor. A covered portion contains stalls in which yard goods and wood and metal crafts are sold. Neighboring enterprises include barber shops, restaurants and cafes, food stores, and a poultry exchange. Further down the road, which is wide enough for a donkey but not for a Jeep, the shops specialize in meat, fish, candy, and pastry. Kitchenware, tools, and other household items are being featured in somewhat more modernized shops. These are increasingly operated by Jews from European countries who sell Israeli-manufactured products. There is a moderate amount of specialization in Acre's *suq*, but much less than in the markets of Nazareth or Jerusalem. The quality of goods is adequate for the peasant and working-class population who are served. For finer products, residents are accustomed to travel to Haifa. However, there are shops along Ben Ami Street in Acre's New City which display the latest fashions in furniture and festival clothing. The pattern of vacationing in Beirut or Europe has been restricted by war and heavy customs duties, but affluent families do travel abroad and manage to bring home souvenirs.

A typical day in Acre's Arab sections is a scene of coming and going by bus and on foot to the market and to bureaus, conducting business, and catching up on personal affairs. Buses come from villages along the Safed and the Naharya-Haifa highways and discharge Arab and Druze families at Farhi Square on Sallah ad-Din Street. Men wear the *kufiya*, which is a white cloth head cover, and they often are clothed in dark jackets and trousers. Traditional robes are disappearing with the passing of the older generation. Women wear light or dark kerchiefs and long dresses of printed cloth. The veil is no longer seen. Children give evidence of modernization as they sport khaki or knit brief garments. The families bring net bags or woven baskets to market, but, unlike tradition, they no longer carry poultry or produce for direct sale. The Labor Federation's marketing cooperative, Tnuva, has enrolled the Arab villages in Israel's widespread trucking system so that products are trucked to wholesale stations, such as Acre's Khan es Shawarda, for distribution to the small shops. Another benefit from membership in the Labor Federation is the Kupat Holim, which is the Sick Fund. Many families come to town to visit prenatal and postnatal clinics, though village services have also been initiated.

Recreation is combined with the conduct of business as the villagers drop by favorite food stands for *felafel*, which are fried cakes made of chick-pea paste, *gazoz*, soda pop, salads, sweetmeats, and coffee. Men may conduct legal transactions over coffee and cigarettes and sometimes alcoholic beverages. They also play backgammon and chetbet at cafes where women and children do not join them. If the market visitor has family members residing in town, then a visit is in order, perhaps for lunch. On major festivals and family celebrations, elaborate preparations are made for visiting and dining. In the evening young people come to enjoy the cinema and to socialize with friends at the cafe or at home.

HOME LIFE AND FAMILY

Domestic life among the Arabs is designed to assure privacy from the outside world, while at the same time it offers much hospitality to family and to strangers under ritualized conditions. The crowded apartments force family members to sleep in all rooms and on the roof during hot summer months. But one room is always made ready for visitors during the daytime and early evening hours. Soon after rising the women of the household remove sleeping mats and bedding to air on the roof (or on the balcony of modern apartments). They wash down the tile floors and set up chairs around the sides of the room that will be used for receiving guests. Some seating is built in stone or cement and covered with cushions of rug wool or sheep skins. More affluent families have inherited massive upholstered chairs of the Turkish period. Poor families provide simple wooden stools with seats of woven rush. Tables also vary in size and in quality. Trays of iron, copper, brass, or tin are more prevalent than Victorian tables. Small stands are inlaid with mother-of-pearl imported from the great bazaars of Damascus or Jerusalem. There are designs on trays and frames on the walls that feature ornamental Arabic calligraphy embodying religious and folk signs and sayings. The quality of carpets and mats varies with the fortunes of the household. Young families have introduced Danish-modern style furniture, which they see in the shops in the New City and in the homes of Jewish friends. There are often debates about the suitability of traditional compared with contemporary apartment housing in terms of the privacy and hospitality each allows.

Coffee-making in a Druze village to display hospitality.

A family's reputation is derived from its ability to provide for guests. On important occasions, such as festivals, weddings, circumcisions, and funerals, many families go into debt to assure an atmosphere of proper behavior which borders on the exaggerated and ostentatious.

Within the family the conversation may be quite personal and heated, but with strangers the emphasis is on the exchange of pleasantries and social ease. The hospitality begins with soft drinks, cigarettes, and candies. Small cups of dark and heavily sweetened coffee are passed by men during a short visit; when there has been considerable feasting, the coffee marks the end of the visit. Fruits in season are served on plates and are often peeled in advance by the host or the women. While men dominate gatherings in the reception room, the women visit among themselves in part of the same room or else in the food preparation area.

Both men and women mingle freely on private family occasions, but separation and seclusion of women takes place when strangers are present. Among Christian families and young couples of all groups, however, there is greater social interaction between male and female hosts and guests, especially if they wish to appear "modern" and are entertaining in more westernized style. Muslim women are most likely to be secluded, but those who have attended parochial school and the higher levels of the government school feel greater freedom to mingle if the situation is modern.

Certain foods are maintained in daily supply by the good homemaker and she preserves seasonal products by drying and pickling. The basic bread is called *pitta*; it is flat and forms an envelope in which meats and salads can be placed for casual snacks. The bread is now baked commercially and is delivered hot and sold almost immediately. Other daily staples include white cheese and yogurt, which is called *lebaniye*. These are delivered to shops through the producers' cooperative, Tnuva, and their quality and price are controlled by government inspectors. Olives are also served with most meals. They are picked in season and pickled in the villages or in wholesale storage places. The oil is highly valued and presses are found in the villages and in town. Vegetables and fruits abound in great variety and their price in season is moderate. Salad items include tomatoes, scallions, cucumbers, and eggplants. Okra, squashes, and beans are boiled and may be combined with tomato paste. Squashes are stuffed with rice, meats, pine-nuts, and flavored with cinamon. Imported foods such as rice and spices are expensive as are beef and lamb; hence they are combined to stretch costs. Fish and poultry are also served and are less expensive, but not as festive as meat. The network of wholesale and retail food outlets assures the distribution of Israeli-grown oranges, lemons, grapefruits, melons, apricots, grapes; the more exotic pomegranates, figs, and dates; and now apples and a variety of nuts. Agricultural extension services have tried to sponsor developments in fruit tree and nut cultivation in the Galilee to supplement the traditional commercial dependence on the olive. The housewife may purchase cakes and cookies from a favorite purveyor in the market or else she will bake special pastries for festive occasions. Desserts are very rich and may include honey, sesame seed oil, almonds, and pistachio nuts, as in *baqlava*. Carbonated beverages and fruit juices are widely served and the bottles exchanged for refills. Coffee, tea, and sugar take up substantial amounts of the household food costs and are central to hospitality. Alcoholic beverages are kept on hand, but are not served to traditional Muslims. There are many local wines, brandy, and *araq*, an anise liquor sold in the stores. Imported whiskeys are very expensive and are served to important westernized guests. Chocolate candies are often brought as house gifts, also flowers which are used as the centerpiece for the home and its company.

Among the Arabs of all sectarian groups, the extended kinship group and kin ties are traditionally valued. Personal identity and economic security are strongly anchored in one's kin group. The wars and enforced separation among families have caused great mental anguish as well as loss of social contact and property transfers in the normal way. Memories of scattered kinsmen linger and great efforts are made to arrange visits over the borders wherever possible. Before the 1967 Six-Day War, while Jerusalem was divided and Bethlehem was under Jordanian administration, Christian families undertook considerable bureaucratic and physical inconvenience to spend Christmas and Easter holidays with relatives. Hovever, Muslims were not admitted by neighboring Arab states for pilgrimages to Jerusalem or to Mecca. The nearby borders with Lebanon remain closed and Syria is unusually hostile. Rendezvous are arranged in Cyprus, but these are expensive and subject to security surveillance because of government anxieties over espionage. There has been considerable illegal reentry into Israel attempted, but, when times are relatively quiet, reunion has been permitted. During periods of guerrilla activity, the police are likely to shoot at infiltrators and to treat them harshly if captured. There was much visiting between Arabs on the West Bank of the Jordan River and the coastal area of Israel after 1967, but security authorities are ever more on the alert for grenade and other attacks and sabotage. When the military government ruled in the Galilee, passports were required for daily trips and overnight visits between villages or towns. This indignity is now over, but resentment lingers and feeds the nationalist arguments of the Communist party. Coalition Labor party members and religious leaders among the Arabs exert pressure from within the government to normalize visiting and property rights of families. The Israeli response is to blame the situation on the intransigence of the neighboring Arab states and the disloyal acts of young Arabs within Israel.

Arab family tradition still honors the elders and is concerned with the maintenance of family status and the transfer of property. Young men about to enter into a marriage contract must provide a *mohar*, which is a bride-price to compensate the father-in-law for the loss of his daughter's service and also for having reared her. Today, the mohar may comprise a year's wages and it is usually raised through family effort and is spent on the couple's housing and furnishings. Young women bring dowries consisting of domestic goods they have sewn and fashioned in the company of their mothers and sisters. It is becoming customary for young male wage-earners to borrow from Labor Federation sources or the banks for housing and for women wage-earners to purchase their household goods in shops.

Male family members are responsible for the reputations of their sisters, moth-

Arab musicians at a reception.

ers, and wives. Arranged marriages used to give preference to the *bint am*, the father's brother's daughter (or patrilineal parallel cousin), which assured close personal and property controls. Urbanization, modernization, and the disruptions due to the wars have reduced this practice of arranged marriage, but marriage within religious and appropriate class-status groups is encouraged by legislation (see later discussion) and by peer-group interaction in activities sponsored by the schools, youth clubs, and political parties. Even where there are instances of cross-ethnic interaction, as at Terra Sancta school, the American Friends Service Committee community center, or the Arab-Jewish summer institute, which is held in Acre, both the elders and the sponsors are cautious to uphold family honor by chaperoning the young women. The newspapers are filled with accounts of male revenge and murders within families of members who bring dishonor.

COMMUNALISM AS UNITY AMIDST DIVERSITY

The Arabs of Acre, as throughout the Middle East, are divided into religious community groups which also have ethnic, political, and cultural traditions. There are sects within Islam and a variety of Christian denominations. The Druzes and Bahai, while not properly Arab, are minority communities with historical linkages to Islam. The religious communities are important sources for personal and group identification both by members and by others in the larger society. In Acre, the Arab religious communities date from the end of the Eastern Roman Empire and the spread of Islam. The attempts of European countries to assert their influence in the eastern Mediterranean have given a nationalistic dimension to Muslim-Christian relations. Arabs view the rise of Zionism and the establishment of the state of Israel in 1948 as an extension of western intrusion in the Middle East. Contemporary intercommunity relations among the Arabs themselves, and also between the Arabs and Jews, are influenced by Israel's governmental policy which recognizes the Arabs as an official minority with cultural and civil rights.

Under Israeli law, the traditional practices of the Turkish and British regimes have been continued whereby religious community officials have authority over personal and family affairs such as marriage, divorce, legitimacy, and inheritance. Intermarriage among Muslims, Christians, and Jews is practically impossible without conversion, and no group supports this. Domestic and community life thus have sectarian limits, despite the growth of secularism and humanism in the country. In Israel, the Religious parties have a major say in coalition governments that are dominated by Labor. Tradition is supported by government institutions, such as the Ministry of Religious Affairs and cabinet posts that fall to Religious party members of the coalition and give them the power of patronage. These have included Social Welfare, Health, and sometimes Interior ministries. There is a section on Arab Minority Affairs in the Ministry of Education and in the Office of Prime Minister.

THE MUSLIM ARAB COMMUNITY

Islam is the dominant religion of the Arabs in Acre, as well as those in Israel and the Middle East. Approximately 6000 Muslims live in Acre and they outnumber the Christians by about three to one. The Islamic community includes families native to the city, many of the village refugees, and most of the bedouin refugees. It includes the leading Arab families of Acre, who direct its institutions, and also the poorest and most crowded slum-dwellers. The political parties and the Labor Federation in Acre are very sensitive to the feelings of the Muslim Arab population. They recognize that while the population does not participate in daily prayer or other religious practices to the extent that their ancestors did, Muslims identify with the religious community and rally to its leadership and institutions when they feel threatened. Government authorities are cognizant of the international basis for Islamic faith and Peoplehood. Both Israeli Jews and Arabs understand that the centers of Islam are rooted in the countries that have declared enmity toward Zionism and Israel. The Saudi Arabians have not permitted Israeli Arabs to make their ritual Pilgrimage, called the *hajj*, to Mecca and Medina. All Arabs resent the fact that the Jews control Jerusalem and the Mosques of al-Aksa and Omar, which are second in rank only to the holy places in Arabia.

Islam is a nonhierarchical religion without a real priesthood, but those who lead community affairs and who are scholars and judges command great respect and influence. In Acre, religious activity among the Muslim Arabs is carried on under the special circumstances of a limited leadership, latent nationalism, and strategies of negotiation with the Jewish and Labor majority. Among the significant Muslim community activities in Acre are the operations of the religious court, (called the *shari'a*), and the charitable foundation (called the *waqf*). The religious court meets regularly at Jazzar Mosque, which is the most important mosque in the district. Its judge is called a *qadi* and this is one of the most prestigious and politically significant positions that an Arab in Acre can attain.

The Israeli Ministry of Religious Affairs, in consultation with other government bureaus, supervises the selection of the *qadi* and the general activities of the religious court. The Arabs cynically claim that politics influences the selection of the religious court judge and that true scholars are lacking, since many of them fled as refugees and others are too nationalistic to meet government tests of approval. The *qadis* of Acre do represent a compromise between local and national accommodation to the Arab minority status in Israel. Arab notables participate in the recommendations, but they acknowledge that the judge must also be acceptable to government authorities. The successful judge spends much time settling the personal affairs of community members, but he is also a focal point for community response to events that affect its condition.

The Muslim Arabs of Acre are represented by a Muslim or Islamic Committee, which also acts as trustee for the funds of the charitable foundation. The Israeli Ministry of Social Welfare participates in decisions concerning waqf expenditures, which must be for public purposes. Most of the Muslim Committee are quite conservative and most funds go for embellishment of the mosques and other ritual matters. More recently, funds have been invested in an orphans' home and in workshops for the disabled. There are plans to improve clubhouses for the elderly and to provide for youth groups. However, the Committee has resisted the pressure of those who would have it invest in business loans and housing. It claims that the funds were gathered before the 1948 period and should be held in escrow for those who are now refugees outside Israel. The Committee also feels that the government, not the waqf, should provide more services for the Arab population as it does for Jewish immigrants. The fact that world Jewish philanthropy through the Jewish Agency sponsors the immigrants, does not satisfy Arab critics. Muslim community leaders court the Religious and the Nationalist political parties when they seek leverage, but they know their fate is linked with the fortunes of the Labor party coalition. They resist open support of the Communist party, which has become the spokesman for Arab grievances and nationalism. Jewish authorities understand the confluence of Arab interests and their use of the multiparty system to further their cause.

Traditional religious practices and regulations among the Muslims have atrophied during the past decades. Polygamy and child marriage have been abrogated by law. Women's rights and freedom of expression for girls have advanced through the schools and activities in the Labor movement. There is a generally secular trend in Israeli society, which relegates religious practice to major rites of passage and to nationalistic expression. Prayer in the mosque takes the form of an old men's club, and on Friday, the Muslim day of worship, few businesses are closed. Labor contracts allocate free time for the major religious festivals, but these are celebrated mainly as family gatherings. Meanwhile, the atmosphere of the Jewish Sabbath and festivals encourages leisure time activity for Arab as well as Jewish workers and those who service them. The daily call to prayer by the muezzin from the minarets has given way to electronic devices and also to radio and television as sources for religious inspiration. This has happened in all the lands of Islam, but the loss of tradition seems accentuated in Israel where the Arabs have become a minority. Greetings are exchanged between the government and religious and community leaders at times of holy festivals. The Muslim Committee, in turn, joins the reception line at Israeli Independence Day celebrations and proclaims loyalty to the state during threats of war.

Class and status differences exist within the Muslim Arab community, particularly between the older city families and some of the village migrants and the bedouin refugees. The city families are more likely to have property that they acquired from the time of the Turks and the British. They are also more likely to have had formal education under the British or through parochial schools and to be engaged in commercial or craft occupations. Under conditions in Israel, Muslim villagers with education, skills, and family support now gain status and power through participation in regional political and religious activities. It is now advantageous to remain in the village since basic education and other services are reaching points of equality with the city. Some city migrants are returning to the village so that their families will lead a more tranquil and traditional life. Commuting services make this possible and the desire to escape urban intergroup tensions makes this desirable.

Muslim refugees from nomadic tribal or peasant groups constitute the poorest and least skilled population, but their potential has increased tremendously. Through the labor movement, they have been recruited to construction work and thus they have earned more money than they have had in the past. They are less bitter about the lack of bureaucratic opportunities than more educated Christians or Muslims since, relatively, they have many advancement possibilities. Leadership in the construction unions and political connections, together with a greater satisfaction with the new life, make such families better citizens in the eyes of the Jewish leaders. Of course, all admit that Arab nationalism could erupt among this group also. The satisfaction may not last more than a generation if the vocational aspirations of youth are raised without being attained. Arab leaders decry a tendency to make them a nation of "hewers of wood and drawers of water" for the Jews. Many Zionists agree that this could corrupt the purposes of the Jewish Homeland.

The influence and experiences of the Muslim Arabs of Acre, at this point, might be contrasted with those of the Druzes and the Bahai, which are very small minority groups. The Druzes seem to be a non-Arab people, whose secret religion derives from Islam. Their local center is on Mount Carmel and in the Galilee, but their national force is in Lebanon and in Syria. The Druzes supported Israel during the 1948 war under a traditional Middle East practice, "My enemy's enemy is my friend." As a result, the Druzes have continued to serve in the Israel Defense Forces and in the border patrols where no Muslim Arab would be expected to risk confronting a kinsman infiltrating over the frontier. Druze society remains more patriarchal than the changing Arab institutions, for women are closely controlled in their villages and seem to exist mainly to bear children annually. Druzes commute to Acre daily to the city market and to the clinics. They are a reminder that the whole Middle East remains a mosaic of mutually antagonistic groups living in a somewhat symbiotic relationship.

The Bahai have their religious centers in Acre and in Haifa, which they established during the nineteenth century in the Ottoman Turkish lands when they fled persecution in Persia. The Bahai faith originated in Islam but became cosmopolitan and humanistic, much in advance of the majority religious cultures of its time. The Bahais have worldwide support and sources of wealth, and pilgrimages bring the faithful from many countries to the tomb of the Baha-Ullah (Glory of God), which is in the Persian Garden, north of Acre. A few dozen Bahai families live in Acre and their name is Irani. They are well thought of because they are peaceable and educated. Some are merchants and others serve in the bureaucracy as teachers and clerks. They have large property holdings which have so far blocked government development plans. They also have identity problems because of their small numbers. Many Bahai have migrated overseas while others have married among Christians, and sometimes Jews or Muslims. Because of their international connections, they are a public relations concern for the government, but they also play a mediational role among Jewish and Arab groups.

CHRISTIAN ARAB COMMUNITIES

The Christian Arab communities of Acre seek to express their interests as Arabs, as religious and political minorities, and as the clients of powerful Christian interests based overseas. The Israeli government must consider public relations in dealing with the Christian Arab communities and also the history of their identification with Arab nationalism. Acre's Christians number a few thousand and they belong to such well-known denominations as Greek Orthodox, Greek Catholic (Malekite), Latin (Franciscan) Catholic, Maronite, and a variety of Protestant congregations. These Christians have a heritage of European influence in the Turkish Empire, whence they established semiautonomous consulates for commercial privileges and extended these to education and to political expansion.

Acre's Christian Arabs are sufficiently small in numbers so that they must unite in common cause with the Muslims against Jewish dominance. In Nazareth and in Jerusalem, where the Christian communities are associated with famous and wealthy religious and pilgrimage centers, there is far greater conflict among the Christian sects and between them and the local Muslims. In Acre, there is a single parochial school, Terra Sancta, and the children come from all the Christian as well as many Muslim families. Christians dominate the leading nationalist political party, the Communists, whose leader is a layman in the Greek Orthodox church. The Israeli authorities distrust the Christian Arabs because many are well educated and quite bitter over the loss of the status they had under the British Mandate. Even in the marketplace, Christian merchants find it difficult to compete with the more modern practices of Jewish immigrant shopkeepers, and they see little future for themselves or for their children here. Christian Arab youth have been active in radical nationalist protest against the Israeli government's policy of using "security" as a rationalization for limiting job opportunities for them.

Religious practices among Christian Arabs in Acre serve to reinforce personal and family identity in a societal sense more than in the spiritual one. The Orthodox and the Catholic churches conduct daily and weekly masses. These are attended mainly by older women, children, and the staffs of parochial schools such as the Dames de Nazareth. At family celebrations, such as christenings and weddings, the churches are filled to overflowing and many guests come from among neighbors and from the villages. Patron saint days, such as Saint George's among the Orthodox and Saint Andrew's among the Greek Catholics, are also occasions for intercommunity participation and celebration. Easter and Christmas are major family festivals, but the center of celebration shifts to Nazareth and to Jerusalem for those families who can afford to travel and who can make this an occasion of reunion with dispersed relatives.

Religious community leadership includes the clergy and leading lay members who participate in councils that handle trust funds and manage other affairs. Native Arab clergymen serve the Orthodox congregations in Acre and in many surrounding villages. They are usually married and have families, and they are sensitive to the sufferings of the local people resulting from the 1948 war and its dislocations. The other churches often have missionary clergymen who are Europeans trained in eastern rites and Arabic culture. Their influence on local congregants depends on their maintaining autonomous behavior toward the government to some extent. It is difficult to be neutral about Arab-Israeli political relations, but the clergy try to take a broad perspective. They develop ways of using influence from overseas in order to mitigate government Arab policy. They strive to control the excesses of nationalism that are present, among youth especially. The government certifies clergymen and so it can eliminate ultra-Nationalists. On the other hand, clergy must speak out against discrimination to maintain the confidence of the membership. The clergy do not participate in political party activities or in the labor movement, but their laymen often do. Secular political and labor movement leadership has become more important than religious community leadership because it has greater leverage to negotiate with the Jewish majority, which needs them in the coalition. Yet Israel is highly sensitive to the Vatican and United Nations connections of local Arab Christian denominations and, like the Turks before them, they try to conciliate, or at least not alienate, the clergy.

Protestant representation is very small among the Christian Arabs, but it has had unique influence in the past on local and international relations. At the time of the Turks, the French and the Austrians supported the Catholics and the Russians protected the Orthodox. The British, the Germans, and the Americans gained entry into the Middle East through Protestant missionary activities. Under the British Mandate, the Christian Arabs benefited much by government employment and many converted to Anglicanism. Alumni of the American University of Beirut provided much needed professional personnel and laid the basis for an Arab nationalism that brought Muslims and Christians together against the Turks and then the Zionists. In Acre the last rallying point among the Protestants was the community center sponsored by the American Friends Service Committee, albeit their activities were oriented toward welfare rather than religion. Missionary Baptists have come to Acre from Haifa and Nazareth and they are making small progress among Arab youth who seek educational and other advances in America. (Jewish authorities have been quick to halt Christian proselytization among alienated European and Oriental immigrant families.) The future of Christianity among the Arabs of Acre is its function as a link with the western world. Otherwise, the traditional groups seek to accommodate to the realities of life in Israel by encouraging the learning of Hebrew language and technical training as Terra Sancta school has recently done.

The relations among Arab religious communities and their accommodation to their minority status in Israel alternates between ritualistic and pragmatic cooperation and traditional rivalry and mistrust. The ethnic mosaic has been put under high pressure since the 1948 Arab-Israeli War, and this can often be seen in Acre as a microcosm. For example, during the early 1950s the Vatican sent a gift of powdered milk and yellow cheese to the government of Israel for the use of Arab refugees. The Israeli Ministry of Foreign Affairs, sensitive to the importance of international Roman Catholic opinion, thanked the donor and turned the matter over to the Ministry of Social Welfare. This ministry, which is often under Orthodox Religious Jewish control, gave the responsibility for distributing the food to local Arab offices. In Acre, the Arab social worker was a Muslim and he felt the gift should go to bona fide refugees on the welfare lists. His advisory committee of clergy and secular leaders generally concurred with this policy. But there was criticism from Latin Catholic quarters (and to some extent the Greek Catholics) since they were clients of the Vatican and most of the refugees were Muslim, including many bedouin. The clergy and the American Friends Service Committee favored an ecumenical position on the distribution of food to Arab refugees, but local and traditional hostilities threatened the spirit of the largesse. In distant villages the sectarian approach won out or else the food was kept in storage to prevent the outbreak of pervasive factionalism. In Acre the Arab refugees did receive their share, but they soon turned it over to the black market as barter for more traditional foods.

Relations among young men and women are another source of friction among traditional sectarian groups, though inroads have been made by intergroup programs sponsored by the American Friends Service Committee and the Prime Minister's Office. Marxist political parties, such as MAPAM with its kibbutz resources, have brought youths together for agricultural work and recreation along with indoctrination. American Friends Service Committee work-camp programs mix Arabs with Jews and European youths. Small numbers of Muslim young women have attended with their brothers as chaperons. At the Arab-Jewish summer institute, which is held annually in Acre by the Prime Minister's Adviser on Arab Affairs, the young women tend to come from a Teachers' Seminary in Haifa and from Oriental programs at the Jewish secondary schools in large cities. Guest lecturers and village hosts generally approve of the activity and the youths are able to express their deep feelings about life in Israel beyond the usual ritualistic etiquette that characterizes the culture.

Dancing, along with the possibility of dating and marriage across religious lines, causes anxieties among both intergroup sponsors and their critics. The American Friends Service Committee had to halt square dancing at its community center. Arab youth clubs emphasize traditional *debka* line dancing, which separates young men and women. The Hebrew circle dance, the *hora*, is allowed because it moves too swiftly to arouse the passions and support may be on the shoulders rather than around the waist. After the successful Arab-Jewish summer camp sponsored by Acre's police, attempts by counsellors to continue social activities were discouraged. Local effort to sponsor a cultural discussion series at a Catholic meeting hall in the Old City has tended to be formalized and without recreational programs that would allow young men and women to interact. One source of inner conflict is that Arab youth models much of its aspirations on the much freer Jewish youth and the world of the cinema and television. Membership in sectarian communities grants identity with the past but it restricts full participation in modern urban societal life.

INDIVIDUAL ADAPTATION AND MOBILITY

Arabs in Acre have responded both innovatively and pragmatically to the transition from old to new ways since the 1948 Arab-Israeli War. Family and sectarian commitments remain strong, but they are not sufficient to enable individuals to realize their search for status and property. They have developed alternative political and social relations with government institutions and personnel. The individuality of choice follows patterns of limited options, as illustrated in the following examples taken from the author's field work.

One leading political and religious leader among the Muslim Arabs comes from a family that had status before the 1948 war. As a young adult he decided to make his future in his native city and to participate in its broadest social and political life. Though his training has been professional and entrepreneurial, he decided that the Labor party coalition offered the greatest potential for power and influence on other aspects of life in this environment. He participated in an Arab party that combined social justice with labor issues and he joined the coalition in the Municipal Council as a Depty Mayor. This leader is a devout Muslim, which is unique for his generation and station in Acre. He was a clerk in the religious court before his political success. Afterwards he set his sights on becoming *qadi*, religious judge in Acre. There were several disappointments, but he finally received the appointment because he had proved his loyalty to the coalition and the government and he had shown a consistent ability to get along with a variety of communal groups and influential individuals.

This political and religious leader demonstrated an interest in cosmopolitan affairs by his activities on the advisory council of the community center sponsored by the American Friends Service Committee. Moreover, his wife, who also came from a traditional family with property and prewar political influence, joined him in community center projects. The young couple thus carried out leadership roles among their peers and extended their relations into the other communal groups in

Acre. They sent their children to Terra Sancta school in order for them to receive a westernized education. The daughters completed their education there, and thus were separated from the refugee children at the government school. The sons, however, were transferred back to the government school when they became older, because it seemed politically expedient for the family to support government institutions and to develop a constituency among these new residents. The wife directed club work for Muslim Arab young women and the husband took charge of rehabilitating a building in the Old City as a service center for the elderly.

These community leaders were prominent in the Acre Rotary Club, where they interacted with other cultivated Arabs and with westernized Jews. They joined in programs that were linked with similar civic groups throughout Israel and those parts of the world influenced by western ideals of international fellowship and good works. The Israeli as well as the international press gave prominence to the Deputy Mayor's pronouncement during the mid-1960s in which he invited President Bourguiba of Tunisia to visit Acre and to see how it is possible for Arabs and Jews to live and work together in peace. But events since the 1967 war have given concern to leaders who aspired to integration. The political coalition persists but as community spokesmen they feel themselves increasingly subjected to international developments beyond their control.

The second leading Muslim Arab in Acre comes from a background in construction work. He has used the strength of his constituency to move up in the ranks of the Labor Federation executive committee and into the Municipal Council, where he would like to be recognized at least as a Deputy Mayor. The labor leader has a gruff manner and readily engages in arguments with his Jewish colleagues over Arab rights. The Jews recall that the leader was an active nationalist in his youth, but they also value his attacks on the communists who have made inroads in the Arab worker vote. The labor leader has been successful in getting the Jews to provide benefits for his followers, and thus feels he has gained more by working within the coalition, although critical of its programs, than by joining the left-wing opposition. He has gained status along with his office, but this is derived almost entirely from the employment situation and potential for semi-skilled Arabs in a boom economy. He is not particularly religious and neither his wife nor his children assist him in his civic activities. He is accepted because the Jews fear that without his leadership there would be more radical Arab nationalism tinged with violence.

The New Communist party is a legal means by which Arabs can confront the Israeli government with its alleged sins against the Arab people. Two leaders within the party in Acre represent diverse backgrounds and methods for accommodating to their situation. The party leader, who has regularly been elected to the Municipal Council, has a background in law and is native to the city. He is active in the affairs of the Greek Orthodox Church and participated in the American Friends Service Committee community center. He was attracted to the Communist party because it espoused integration for Arabs and Jews in the Middle East and resolved to end nationalist conflict. Most Jews have left the movement, since it has become identified with Arab nationalism. Membership thus appeals to Arab youth who are disillusioned with their minority situation. The party leader is interrogated regularly by security police and is jailed occasionally. His wife was accused of leading the Terra Sancta school pupils in a nationalist demonstration in 1961, which resulted in street riots with Oriental Jews. Officials consider the Communist party to be hostile to the existence of the Jewish state, but their members have used the techniques of public demonstration rather than bombing and individual forms of sabotage.

The disciple of the Communist party leader is a migrant from a nearby village who supports his family by working with his hands. His political philosophy is based on social justice for both Arabs and Jews. He does not seek office, but rather has improved his technical skills to become self-sufficient as a mechanic. Despite his political allegiance to the opposition party and its nationalist connotation, his workshop obtains many contracts from neighboring agricultural settlements and transportation groups. He belongs to the craftsmen's cooperative within the Labor Federation, even though he is critical of its bureaucracy and services. He and his large family live in an old house dating from Turkish and perhaps Crusader times. He has participated in Protestant church activities and the American Friends Service Committee community center. Somehow, he has combined a controversial political interest with a trade that is much in demand. In modest fashion he seems to thrive on these achievements and to prepare his sons to continue these ways.

From the individual's point of view, kinship obligations are both a help and a constraint on upward mobility. In a family of Christian Arab refugees from a city in the Galilee, its several members have grown up around a strong mother and they have pooled their resources to enable each member to achieve some potential. The eldest son is reported to be living in Kuwait, where Palestinian refugees provide needed skills in the petroleum fields. Another son is proud to be a worker and to participate in Acre's Labor Federation. Some brothers have taken semi-skilled employment, either because they have not progressed in education or else because they claim there is discrimination against them for white-collar jobs. One daughter stays home to help with domestic activities. Another daughter has become a school teacher, but she feels unhappy at the long and difficult commuting time to the village where she was assigned. Another son has advanced his education in industrial arts and he maintains himself as a teacher in the local secondary school. In addition, he has bought up residential property in the Mandate New City to rehabilitate and to rent to tenants. A younger son has thought about migrating overseas because he is attracted to western styles of life. But he has made progress as a clerk in a bank and he has made a decision to live near his family and friends.

This family is hospitable and is well thought of in its neighborhood. But it has suffered from its dislocation in 1948, its loss of property, and especially its separation from the eldest son. During the 1967 war period, the family sensed prejudice against them from their Jewish neighbors. It has become difficult for them to reconcile pride and a desire for broad interpersonal relations with current tendencies which are dividing the society.

Withdrawal to Arab village life is a response made by some persons who find the pressures of nationalism in an urban setting intolerable. One professional worker after receiving his education overseas left his village for employment in Acre. But he was uncomfortable in the atmosphere of the refugees and he chafed at the political intrigues of the Jewish immigrant parties and their Arab supporters. He chose the integrationist Marxist party, MAPAM, rejecting the ultranationalist Communists. He removed his family to his native village where he is able to commute to work in the Acre district. He enjoys traditional family life and participation in local kinship and community affairs. He recognizes the importance of dealing with the political structure, but he prefers to separate this from his personal life. He grows impatient for the restoration of Arab property and dignity, but he has not approved the increased guerrilla activity by young men in the area. The villages have grown in prosperity but individual members respond variously to the call of nationalism.

The ultimate form of withdrawal from the minority situation is to leave the country. The government realizes that this is an indication that intergroup relations have not fulfilled their promise in every case, but they also favor emigration in order to reduce pent-up tensions. The Arabs claim such policy is purposeful in order to maintain a Jewish elite. Christian families are more likely to migrate to western countries where their kinsmen have settled successfully since the Turkish period. Muslims consider opportunities in underdeveloped Arab countries, but there is discrimination against Palestinians and these lands are distant from the familiar eastern Mediterranean coast.

In one educated Muslim family, the father lived with the memory of his career as a constable under the British Mandate. He had several sons who sought professional and technical positions such as medicine, engineering, accounting, and teaching. None of these sons found success in the Acre district and claimed they were discriminated against because they were Arabs. Some did not make a strong enough commitment to the political coalition party. Others were denied security clearance because they participated in the 1961 Terra Sancta school demonstration. The family had kinsmen and some property in Jordan, so they applied to the Israeli authorities for exit visas and set forth as bitter exiles. It is not known how the family fared after the 1967 war, but the sons were sufficiently westernized so that they might eventually seek homes in Europe, Canada, or the United States. They have certainly rejected any notions that would identify them with the mass of Arab refugees born of the Palestinian conflict.

INCREASED ARAB ALIENATION SINCE 1967

Trends toward Arab-Jewish integration were reversed during May 1967, when neighboring Arab states threatened to annihilate Israel. In June, the Jews gained a stunning victory in the Six-Day War and extended their occupation of Arab territories, including Jerusalem. On the eve of the conflict local Arab leaders expressed public loyalty to Israel through the Muslim Committee and the Labor Federation.

However, some Jews maintain that Arab youths jeered them and that lists had been drawn up for massacre and booty. Such accusations confirm the Arabs' feelings that first-class citizenship for them in Israel is impossible. They report that, especially in neighborhoods of mixed housing in the New City, they were insulted and even assaulted. Once more they sought refuge behind the walls of Acre. When they emerged, they rejected all plans for housing them in quarters that were dominated by Jewish immigrants.

Israeli government security forces observed Arab nationalists closely during the 1967 period and they detained some Communists for public safety. After Jewish victory and evidence that no Israeli Arab disloyalty had occurred, all detainees were released and it was thought that a new era of Arab-Jewish reconciliation was at hand. But the Jewish majority failed to recognize that integration works best among status equals. Local Arabs were bitterly disillusioned by the ineptness of the Arab armies. They did not want patronage from the Jews either. Arab youths sought new identity in a Palestinian national movement. Events outside the city of Acre once more determined its destiny.

A few years after the 1967 war, the image of Acre as a model for Arab-Jewish relations was shaken by several incidents of local Arab involvement in violence against the Jewish population. These were different from the border incidents that had been prevalent in previous decades and which had limited local repercussions. During the autumn of 1969, several apartment houses in Haifa were detonated, which resulted in the death of the Jewish occupants. Tensions, which had already been aggravated by incidents involving airplane sky-jacking, bombings in public places in Tel Aviv and Jerusalem, and the ambush of a school bus in the Galilee, crossed the threshold for Acre at midnight in November 1969. A passenger car carrying young Arab men halted suddenly at the city's only traffic light near the crossroads of the New City. The vehicle lurched, triggering a violent explosion. This awakened the neighborhood and brought the police, who apprehended three youths, two from the Old City and one from a village. They said they were on their way to Haifa on a mission for the Palestinian underground movement and stated that they had grenades and dynamite in their possession.

The incident was shocking because neighborly trust had been violated in the maelstrom of nationalism, and was considered much more serious than the 1961 demonstration of Communist-led secondary school pupils. Jewish youths marched on the Old City for revenge and, as in the past, the police held them in check. The Arab youths confessed to the police that their action had been a response to their kinsmen from the West Bank of the Jordan, who had visited them and chided them because they had material prosperity in Israel while their brethren were fighting as commandoes. The national press noted that these were not Communist Party members with cosmopolitan ideologies. Rather, they were young men in search of identity, in the tradition of Arab Peoplehood. Both Jews and Arabs understood this need as a basis for violent action. They wondered how long it would be possible for the city and the country to sustain such conflict. Daily life continues to bring the ethnic groups together on the streets, in the marketplace, and in the bureaus. The political coalition promotes the city's development and the police maintain domestic tranquility. Services are performed, but the possibilities for feelings of community in Acre based on intergroup relations are increasingly remote.

The 1973 Arab-Israeli War has furthered local polarization though the coalition government has been sustained. The Arabs view Jewish military might as less invincible and they are impatient for a solution to the Palestinian problem. The Jews grieve over their many dead and maimed and they feel that the world no longer understands their need for a secure Homeland.

4 / Ashkenazi Jews from Europe

European Jews are called Ashkenazim after a Hebrew designation for Germany. The concept has been extended to include Jews who migrated from the Western Roman Empire into Germany and then to central and eastern Europe. Their basic language became Yiddish, a Germanic dialect interspersed with words of the ancient Semitic Hebrew tongue, which is written with Hebrew characters. The spoken Hebrew of Israel uses a Sephardi (i.e., Spanish-Mediterranean), inflection. Jews from Europe with formal religious education are able to communicate with Jews from the Mediterranean and the Middle East after some practice. The religiously educated Jews have superior ability in written composition in Hebrew because they are familiar with biblical and rabbinical texts. This enables them to qualify readily for clerical occupations in Israel's institutions. Secular Jews from Europe, who have been educated in technical and professional studies in the modern national languages of their native lands, attend intensive Hebrew language courses (called *ulpanim*), in order to take high level positions in Israel.

Ashkenazi Jews control the status and power structure of cities like Acre and the institutions of the larger society. Nineteenth century Europe was the source of Zionist ideology, a political movement that was an amalgam of Jewish religious messianism, Marxist socialism, and territorial nationalism. The leaders of Israel value the technical and analytical skills and the westernized culture that European Jewish immigrants can bring to the country. Government policy seeks to keep western immigration high and to assimilate the Jews from Arab lands to the social-democratic and the technological values dominant in the culture of European Jews. They fear an increase in "levantinism" if Arab or Oriental Jewish populations come to dominate.

European Jews constitute about one-fourth of the population of Acre and they dominate its major institutions. But Arabs and Oriental Jews are increasing their numbers and their influence since they have high birthrates and their in-migration has been continuous. European Jewish families are small—two children is the norm—and they tend to leave Acre for more westernized suburbs when they become middle class. Leaders hope that the recent Russian immigration will reinforce local Ashkenazi and westernized cultural influence, but this migration is being directed to more recently designated development towns rather than to Acre.

REFUGEES FROM THE HOLOCAUST

There are areas of similarity between the pioneers of Israel and the more recent European migrants, but they differ greatly in their approaches to settlement in the Jewish Homeland and their involvement in its institutions. Both groups suffered from pervasive anti-Semitism in Europe, but it was the pioneers who took the initiative to leave the ghettos and to establish new institutions in a far away and hostile land, then under Turkish, and later under British, domination. The refugees from Nazism and Communism, in contrast, are welcomed to a modernized Israel by brethren who take credit for having wrested the countryside from an Arab enemy and turning it into modern agricultural and urban settlements. The pioneers have a more communal approach to the development of Israel. They try to help the refugees overcome their mistrust of institutions, which comes from an overdependence on them and frustrations with their complexity. For their part, the refugees feel both gratitude and uneasiness in the development city of Acre. They wish to shield their children from the memories of events in Europe while at the same time they romanticize nostalgic memories of prewar life in their native homes. The Zionist and government institutions acknowledge that they must work hard to bring together Jews from Europe and the Middle East and to weld them into a community.

An event of major importance to the identity of the Ashkenazi immigrants in Acre (observed during fieldwork) was the celebration of the twentieth anniversary of the defeat of Nazi Germany and the release of the Jewish remnant from the concentration camps. The Israeli government planned for nationwide religious memorials combined with patriotic testaments. The radio and the press produced vignettes of Jewish experiences in the ghettos and the death camps of Nazi Europe. They also issued statements from Allied soldiers who had participated in the rescue. There was special recognition of the role of the Palestinian Jewish Community, which had sponsored the Jewish Brigade during World War II, over the opposition of the British and the Arabs. In Acre's Municipal Cultural Center, husbands and wives came to recite the prayer for the dead and to listen to poetry and speeches from the period they knew so well in suffering, but also in deliverance. The ceremony was conducted in Hebrew, which signified that these immigrants were now acculturated to their new homeland, and that defeat had turned to victory.

During this celebration, the remembrance of the Nazi persecution of the Jews was brought to the attention of Israeli youth through the schools and the youth clubs of various political parties. The emphasis was placed on the lesson that such destruction shall never be repeated. The European experience was closely paralleled with Israel's ability to overcome Arab enemies who also want to destroy the Jews. Teachers who had fought against the Nazis and their local fascist supporters recounted experiences of valor under extreme odds. Jewish youths from European and Middle Eastern origins were urged to train for inevitable struggle with those who opposed their existence. Their parents were refugees but the new generation would take up the spirit of the pioneers of Israel.

The saga of the Weiss family is presented here to illustrate the institutional and generational ramifications of leaving Europe to establish a new home in Acre, Israel. Moshe and Hannah Weiss had grown up in a small town in Rumania where overt fascism was replacing the uneasy tolerance of the old Austro-Hungarian Empire and communism in neighboring Russia threatened to take over. The Jewish couple opened a small dry goods shop and developed good relations with their Gentile (non-Jewish) neighbors. After the Nazis overran their region they were interned, but fortunately not in the infamous camps that destroyed six million Jews.

At the end of World War II they were pessimistic about reviving their life in Europe and they joined the streams of other Jews on the way to Palestine. Their period of transit came as the Iron Curtain fell over eastern Europe and the birth of Israel followed a bitter war with the Arabs. They traveled through central Europe to a Mediterranean port as house parents for a group of Jewish youth, organized by Zionist emissaries. The group landed in Haifa and was recruited to settle in the abandoned Arab city of Acre and to serve in the security forces. The Weiss' were thrilled to be in the Jewish Homeland, but they were fearful of the resident Arabs and found the oriental atmosphere of Acre strange. The group was assigned an apartment in the Mandate New City where they shared all facilities. For the Weiss', this meant a single bedroom together with the two young daughters who had been born during the migration journey.

The Weiss' learned how to get along with diverse neighbors and to use the local institutions to become more self-sufficient citizens in Acre. The young companions interceded with the social welfare bureau to provide a shopkeeper's license for Mr. Weiss. The housing bureau offered larger apartments only in remote immigrant quarters, so the Weiss' learned to exchange abandoned Arab apartments with neighbors on their own initiative. They became important leaders in the Ashkenazi religious congregation that was forming. They were active in the social life of the central synagogue, which was located in a former Arab warehouse nearby. They became mediators in the many quarrels that took place among neighbors of diverse ethnic origins and under the great pressures of transition and poverty. They began slowly to learn Hebrew and to meet Arabs in the marketplace and at the shop. They saved their funds in a savings association subsidized by the government toward permanent housing.

As the years passed, the Weiss' daughters contributed to the family income through work, and they enlarged their social networks through new friends and fortuitous marriages. One daughter married into the family that owned the textile factory in which she worked. The new in-laws were influential in Religious party affairs, which brought additional benefits and pleasures to the parents. Together, the families purchased apartments in a developed section that had once been a swamp. This area was destined to become the center for the New City of Acre; a new Ashkenazi central synagogue was dedicated at one end of the site and a new shopping center with a fountain in its public area dominated the other end. From their balcony, the Weiss' enjoyed watching men walking to synagogue in the morning while children cycled to school and housewives came with net shopping bags to sample the produce at a new supermarket. The Weiss' celebrated the Sabbath and festivals in proximity to their children and now their grandchildren.

They regretted that the new generation had not kept up with all the religious observances, but the youth were respectful and loving. The first granddaughter would soon enter military training, which made the Weiss' proud of this family contribution to the Jewish people. Although they found retirement life in Acre much different from Europe, it was also an improvement on the refugee city they had first encountered on arrival.

ETHNIC LINKAGES AND DIFFERENCES

The European migrants and pioneer community leaders have much in common culturally but the heritage of Ashkenazi separatism poses problems in terms of the goals of the development city to integrate all residential groups. The refugee mentality is suspicious, self-seeking, pragmatic, and demanding and therefore, appeals to Zionist ideology generate only a limited response. European immigrants were not always exposed to social democratic institutions except perhaps in Czechoslovakia. They had learned to cope with fascism and communism either through ultraconformity and dependence or else through intrigue and subterfuge. Some found solace in religious faith. Others rejected socialism and other governmental controls, thus placing themselves at odds with Labor party ideology when exposed to it in Israel. Yet most recognized the strength of the General Federation of Labor and its leaders in the government and institutions of Israel, so they were drawn to its ranks. The European Jewish immigrants preferred their own associations, although they acknowledged Oriental Jews as brothers during both groups' assimilation to common institutions in Israel. They were willing to be neighbors to the Arabs if they would agree to peace.

The Ashkenazim progressed in development towns like Acre because they received preferential treatment, which is called *proteksia*. Veteran leaders empathized with their European Yiddish culture and sympathized with the hardships they had endured in Europe. They went out of their way to help them obtain shopkeeper licenses and office jobs. This was bitterly resented by Oriental Jews and Arabs, who were more likely to be given laboring assignments by the bureaucrats. Eventually, the Oriental Jews and Arabs turned the tables on the Europeans as they came to outnumber them. Oriental domination, in turn, accelerated the exodus of veteran settlers and Europeans from Acre to the suburbs.

European immigrants to Acre were divided in identity according to national backgrounds, educational resources, and the value they placed on tradition. Scholarship was a source of status, especially in the religious communities. Lithuanian and Polish Jews felt themselves superior in training to Jews from Rumania, and they tended to dominate the religious institutional structure and the school system as well. The founders of the Labor Federation were also more likely to have come from the earlier waves of migration from Russia or Poland, and this political leadership was transmitted to later migrants from the same national origins. The Rumanian Jews as a group had come through Nazi domination of Europe better than most Polish or Russian Jews, who survived only if they had escaped to Siberia. The Rumanians, thus, were more numerous and more confident as they settled in development towns like Acre, and they began bitter struggles to gain predominance in the bureaucracy. The Poles maintained power only by making agreements with Arab and Oriental Jewish voters. Eventually, as North African Jews came to outnumber all other ethnic groups, they took over the leadership of the Labor Federation and several municipal bureaus.

The economic assets of European migrants also varied with their national backgrounds and experiences under Nazi and, later, Communist regimes. Jewish survivors from Czechoslovakia and Hungary were able to repossess some property between the period of Nazi defeat and Communist takeover. Restitution was paid by West Germany to individuals from many national backgrounds who could prove they had been forced into slave labor or show they had had property confiscated by the Nazis. The Israeli government helped these immigrants to press their claims and their small gains furthered development goals of the regions where they settled. For instance, the immigrants helped foster the private housing market and they invested in businesses that produced consumer goods, including some for export, according to government plans. While many of these families moved away when they became successful, those who stayed benefited from the status they received in Acre.

NEW ALIGNMENTS THROUGH RELIGIOUS ACTION

Traditional values remain strong in development cities like Acre. Both the veteran settlers and the immigrants believe that their presence helps to assure the unity of the Jewish People, who are called '*Am Yisrael*. Religious action is a force for intergroup relations and an instrument for individuals and groups to attain institutional power. The Ashkenazi groups who are each a minority in numbers find they must form coalitions with other traditionalists and also with secularists in order to gain their objectives. For example, they are willing to join Labor in the Municipal Council in opposition to the Communists. In this, the religious Ashkenazim must also acquiesce to the exclusion of the ultra-Nationalists, who often support tradition but who are bitter enemies of Labor. The Religious parties and the Labor parties are rivals for the votes of Sephardi-Oriental Jews. They might be expected to support the Religious parties, but they are resentful of Ashkenazi domination of the Bureau of Religious Affairs, of rituals, and of the interpretations of Jewish customs. Oriental Jews turn to Labor parties because this grants them influence in the spheres of employment, housing, and other essential services. Those who are alienated both from the Religious and Labor parties join the ultra-Nationalists who support tradition and also take a strong anti-Arab position; the latter appeals to Jews from Middle Eastern countries. The Ashkenazi religious leaders, in order to maintain their position both in their political parties and in the coalition, have made concessions to Sephardi-Oriental rituals and they are granting leadership positions to Middle Eastern Jews in the parties and the bureaucracies that they control.

The public celebration of Simchat Torah (Rejoicing in the Law), represents an attempt by religious leaders of the Bureau of Religious Affairs and by the synagogues to bring unity out of diversity of tradition. The festival marks the end of eight days of Succoth, a calendrical period that represents the shelters in which the Children of Israel of the Old Testament sojourned while wandering through the Wilderness on their way to the Promised Land. It also celebrates the fall harvest and commemorates the conclusion of a cycle of reading from the Torah (the Five Books of Moses, which is the Law).

Ritually observant Jews make the shelters ("booths") out of palm fronds and families dine there. At morning prayer services, they carry a palm branch entwined with sprigs of myrtle and willow (called a *lulav*), and a citron (called an *ethrog*). They say a prayer of thanksgiving for "former" rains in this season and beg for "later" rains in the winter to assure abundant harvest for the spring (when other festivals take place).

As observed in 1965 by the author, the intercommunal celebration of Simchat Torah in Acre was held after the religious services in the communal synagogues was extended by an assembly of the congregations in the central Ashkenazi synagogue. The men and youths carried with them their communal Scrolls of Law, which were wrapped in velvet or encased in silver and mounted with crowns and bells. The children wore the blue and white uniforms of religious youth groups and they formed a procession to the headquarters of the Bureau of Religious Affairs. Trucks with klieg lights bore teenagers who sang and danced en route. A large audience was drawn to the platform set up before the Bureau. The rabbis and municipal officials welcomed the participants through amplified sound-speakers. They turned the program over to cantors from communal synagogues, who rendered traditional chants in their unique fashion. Meanwhile, the younger generation performed Israeli chain dances and ring dances continuously on the outskirts of the assembly.

The possibilities for religious integration among the immigrants are limited by their communal needs. Public celebrations are institutionalized through politically inspired objectives, to make a show of strength against secularists. When the Ashkenazim of Acre laid the cornerstone of their new central synagogue, the Sephardim wondered when their turn might come. Ultimately, they did build an attractive building at the opposite end of the field where Acre's new center is developing. But communal congregations persist because they are more intimate and less costly. There was no public celebration of Simchat Torah the year that the Ashkenazi rabbi was out of town visiting relatives who lived in more famous religious centers. The rabbi noted that he had not been too successful in developing a religious academy (called a *yeshivah*), which would alter Acre's image—currently known as the city of Jazzar's Mosque or the city of the Crypt of Saint John. Sephardi rabbinical leadership is even more fragmented, and competition comes from the Religious parties who seek to gain the support of the new generation.

Amalgamation of Ashkenazi and Sephardi-Oriental ritual is taking place in a new congregation formed by the religious youth movement and guided by leaders in the Religious parties and the Bureau of Religious Affairs. The format of Sabbath religious services follows the innovations of the Israeli Defense Forces. The young congregation has been given the use of a chapel on the site of a large housing estate donated by the British Zionist philanthropist, Sir Isaac Wolfson. Some teachers from the religious schools support this movement by their active participation and it is received with gratitude by the youths. While kinship and communal ties continue to characterize traditional life in Acre, the new generation seeks an Israeli identity. This is further evidenced by the fact that one in four Jewish marriages in Acre is between an Ashkenazi and a Sephardi-Oriental. The marital trends have been accelerated especially since the Six-Day War as both groups participated in the defeat of the Arabs.

LOCALISM AND MOBILITY

Life in Acre provides European Jewish immigrants with the means for mobility. Those who have the capacity to utilize its institutions successfully rise in class and power. The decision to remain in Acre is influenced by a family's continuing need for local support and status and the pressures or opportunities perceived in the world outside. Parents usually project their aspirations for status and mobility onto their children, but the new generation is increasingly influenced by institutional leaders to value national policies and interests. The directions of personal and group mobility are influenced by the Jewish experiences in Europe and the value placed on religious tradition and kinship ties. The following examples drawn from field work in Acre illustrate the interplay of events and institutional structures on individual achievement and decisions.

A successful contractor has gained his position in the community through participation in religious and political affairs and the manipulation of minority and marginal associations for his purposes. The family, comprising husband and wife, two sons and a daughter, came to Acre as refugees from Czechoslovakia. The parents were the sole survivors of a group submitted to the Nazi occupation and later they could not abide the restrictions introduced by the Communists. After arriving in Israel, the father, who knew how to work with his hands, soon organized Arab laborers into a construction team to contract for small projects. He was well educated in Jewish religious tradition and he made a place for himself in Acre's Ashkenazi community by leading a discussion group in the central synagogue. However, he preferred to remain a leader in a small central European congregation, which was affiliated with a minor Religious party. He thus led their ballot and gained a seat in the Acre Municipal Council in the coalition. He also gained support from Sephardi Jews because he brought them into official positions in the party, which led to employment for them in the Bureau of Religious Affairs.

The contractor's major undertaking was the construction of an apartment complex at the center of Acre's New City. Immigrant families who had received German restitution payments purchased individual apartments and rented retail shops facing the main street of the city. This enterprise provided the contractor with his own housing in a desirable location and it served the city's development plans, which sought private capital and initiative for this center.

The family observes religious traditions and is hospitable in its ample and modern apartment. The children have graduated from local religious schools and youth groups. They have now reached the age of career decision, which is likely to be oriented toward a profession. They are also close as a family (because they are religious and because there are no other members around).

The family senses that its status in Acre is provincial. In terms of religious affairs, they would prefer to live in a more intellectually stimulating environment, but they have many conservative views. The sons and the daughter have been sent to academies and a university for religious Jewish studies. They are prepared to become teachers, but have set their sights on medicine and engineering. The family decries the Polish and Rumanian factionalism and control of both religious and political institutions in Acre. They do not wish to see the North African Jews obtain ultimate domination. They see Middle Eastern Jews as requiring guidance and assimilation to the levels of religious culture provided by European Jews. The Arabs are viewed as enemies and alien to the objectives of the Jewish Homeland. The parents recognize the limitations of their family resources and their dependence on Acre's diverse groups and institutions for success. They have prepared their children for a more cosmopolitan life, but the children's decision will be influenced by their feeling of closeness to their parents.

Another example of interplay between localism and mobility is provided by a municipal official who is considered a veteran settler in Acre, yet who basically shows the impact of the ghetto and European anti-Semitism to a degree that unites him to the postwar immigrants. The official has held leadership positions in the majority Labor party, MAPAI, but he has been unable to reconcile the Rumanians or the North Africans to his Polish faction. He performs a public function as a civil servant and he carries a somewhat patronizing air of noblesse oblige which he has inherited from experiences with British army leadership in Palestine during World War II. He bears the marks of a ghettoized colonial while he identifies with British cultural institutions, and this makes his status in Acre unfulfilling to himself.

The relationship between the veteran settlers of Acre and the British Mandate was illustrated during a local celebration of the 25th anniversary of the Battle of Britain (observed during the 1965 field work). The municipal official and a colleague who represented a war veterans' group, hosted British consulate officials at the Acre Cultural Center. This local veterans' chapter had lost membership as families left Acre and its environs for the large cities of Haifa, Tel Aviv, and Jerusalem. Two dozen couples from Naharya and the Haifa suburbs attended together with a few local youths. The program consisted of British war films and a reception. The English language was used, but translations into Hebrew were necessary for some of the wives and for children who were present with their families. The reception moved to the tourist cafe on Acre's seashore, where the British Consul tendered an invitation to his host to visit him in his home in Tel Aviv's suburbs.

The municipal official maintains an uneasy balance between loyalties and anxieties. He recognizes the contribution that large numbers of Jewish migrants from Middle Eastern countries can make to Israel, but fears levantinism if they cannot be assimilated to western values. He would prefer that the Religious parties have less control over governmental institutions, yet he acknowledges the historical importance of religious tradition in uniting the Jewish people in the face of religious and political persecution. He admires British concepts of order and dignity, but he has bitter memories about the White Paper of 1939, which closed the doors of Palestine to European Jews who were being engulfed by the Nazis. He is a fervent Jewish nationalist who supports the more moderate Labor party because its leaders pioneered the major institutions of the state. His family is assured an adequate living in Acre and opportunity to enjoy its modest social life. However, he has sent his son to a private school near a metropolis in order to acquire more rigorous academic and professional training. As a sabra, his son is free of ghetto feelings and colonial experiences. It is the desire of his parents to emancipate him also from the immigrant atmosphere of Acre.

A worker who was once active in Acre's Communist party illustrates the effects of coping with the aftermath of the European holocaust and searching for humanistic values suitable for modern Jewish people. As a young man he was taken by the Nazis and the rest of his family were killed. He was liberated by the Red Army and he gratefully gave his allegiance to Russia and the Communist party. Many European Jewish immigrants to Israel admired the strength of the Soviet Union but most feared it and preferred Israel's orientation to the United States, where American Jewish influence had helped secure the birth of the state and its development. This presented a conflict in values and orientations to these immigrants. The small Communist party attracted dissidents who resented the power of the Labor party and who opposed its policy of rapprochement with West Germany. The Communist party was also attractive to Arabs because it claimed to have Russia's sympathy toward a peaceful solution to Arab-Jewish nationalist conflict. This further repelled the immigrants who were once Russian sympathizers.

Being a Communist in Labor-dominated Acre was difficult, and there were many incidents of violence during strikes and sympathetic demonstrations for Arab refugees. The Jewish worker participated in his labor union, which was in a ceramics factory operated by a kibbutz. He felt that the union provided him with an opportunity to reveal the hypocrisy of the Labor establishment. The Communists criticized the Labor Federation's investments in the cement and steel industries in the Haifa Bay area in partnership with government and private capital. This position was not too remote from that of the ultra-Nationalists, but the latter party had a strong anti-Arab position and was suspicious of Russian motives in the Middle East.

Eventually the Jewish workers in the Israeli Communist party, including those in the local branch in Acre, recognized that they felt alien to the policies of the Soviet Union in Europe and the Middle East. During the 1950s Jewish cultural and professional leaders in Russia were liquidated under Stalin. At that time public trials were being held in Poland and Czechoslovakia in which Jewish Communists were denounced and eliminated. It appeared to Israel's Jews, including the Communists, that anti-Semitism had not been resolved by the Communist party, and that the policies resembled those of nineteenth-century Russia under the Czars. The U.S.S.R.'s rationalization that only Zionist Jews were being persecuted became a self-fulfilling prophecy when, after Stalin's death, crowds of once-assimilated Russian Jewish youths in Moscow made the religious festival of Simchat Torah their symbol of unity with the Jewish People and began to demand exit visas to Israel. The final test of the Communist party in Israel came when open Soviet support was given to Egypt and other enemies of Israel. Arab nationalists in Acre came to dominate the party and the Jews withdrew. The fear that preceded the Six-Day War in 1967, and the elation over the reunification of Jerusalem under Jewish control after 2000 years brought nearly all Jews together in a realization that they must not be clients of foreign powers.

This ex-Communist worker now spends much time on his balcony sipping tea as he denounces the perfidity of great nations and the institutional leaders of Israel. He spends time with his neighbor, a worker of Sephardi background, building additional rooms to their apartments, which were once an Arab villa. They watch their children advance from the public kindergarten through the schools where they learn Hebrew and Jewish history. They are proud that their sons are interested in technical training and that they can advance this training in the military service. The neighbors' wives exchange child care and they help one another economize by shopping in the Old City. The worker muses that peace with the Arabs must come through neighborly discussion and negotiation, not through foreign intervention. Meanwhile, he supports Israel's policies of military strength and self-sufficiency. As he takes an evening walk with his wife and son, the worker finds his daily life and associations reasonably satisfying. He has tried to solve the problems of the world but the conflicts have disenchanted and embittered him.

Since he migrated to Acre from Rumania, a successful engineer has spent much time trying to convince the leaders and the public that the history of the city is its greatest resource. He is a member of the ultra-Nationalist party (Likud), which places him in opposition to the Labor coalition. This somewhat limits his ability to convince the Municipal Council to adopt his suggestions about promoting international tourism. He would like to create new names for streets in Acre's Old City by honoring such figures as Marco Polo and the Norse King Sigurd, who were associated with the Crusader period seven centuries ago. The engineer has gained the cooperation of the Acre Rotary Club to sponsor essay contests and discussions about the city's history. He has amassed valuable maps and prints from archives in Jerusalem and overseas and has had copies on display in a new historical museum in Acre's Old City.

The engineer has been fanatical and has brought valuable public relations to Acre, but he has not been able to convince the working class or its leaders that the destiny of the city is to become a living museum. The Arabs prefer a fundamental restoration of their houses and suitable employment for their income source. The planning officials in the Municipality place highest priority on creating industrial and commercial zones in the New City. Projects for restoration and tourist facilities sponsored by the Old Acre Development Corporation have received limited local support. The engineer criticizes them for lacking authenticity. Most of Acre's residents take a pragmatic approach to the city's development and place little faith in the romance of history. The engineer is trying to show them that an appreciation of history and the exploitation of its symbols can create a feeling of identity among residents, particularly the new generation. He hopes this might curb the suburban exodus by those who consider themselves to be successful.

A young refugee from the concentration camps advanced his career in Acre and moved his family from an Oriental ghetto out to the garden suburb, Naharya. Since his parents had perished along with most Jews from the Polish ghettos, he found new family ties through his wife who was from Rumania. The husband and wife were Zionists and they worked diligently with the youth of Acre to infuse them with idealism and patriotism. The refugee became a sergeant in the police force after a training period that brought veterans and immigrants together. He conceived a project to develop juvenile delinquency prevention programs among school dropouts in Acre. His discussion groups and day camps were attended mainly by Oriental Jewish and Arab youths. They were exposed to Jewish and Arab counselors who were to act as role-models. Educators and social workers cooperated, though they were skeptical about the paramilitarism of the program. Municipality officials were generally enthusiastic and gave strong support. The sergeant was somewhat of a hero to the children and their families.

Promotion came with the success of the juvenile program and a ready move out of Acre. The policeman became commander of a district in the Western Galilee. He was offered a political office in Acre, but he turned this down because he did not wish to become embroiled in factionalism. He preferred to professionalize and to carry on civic activities in a more Europeanized and middle-class environment. His wife and children were well prepared to move to Naharya in order to make new social contacts. They would not be too far from their relatives in Acre and, besides, many successful families from Acre were now located in Naharya. The family acquired a substantial apartment overlooking the Mediterranean Sea, after they sold their property in Acre. They felt confident that they would be accepted in the new community because of the talents they could offer. They did not feel it necessary to join in the cafe life and concerts that attracted the upper-middle-class elites of Naharya.

The foregoing cases illustrate that Acre has indeed provided a refuge for its Jewish immigrants from Europe. They have been able to recuperate from the tyranny of the Nazis and the Communists in a land of their own. The remnants of their family life have been gathered together in ways that emphasize strong dedication to the future of the Israeli-born generation. In Acre, the basic necessities for home life and work have developed over the decades. The children have become Israelis through the national orientations of local institutions. The parental generation recalls Europe with mixed feelings. Even though the Jews were a disadvantaged minority in the countries of the Diaspora, they felt that the civilization in those countries was worth emulating. In Acre, Israel, the oriental atmosphere is alien; however, it is necessary to live and to work with Jews from all lands to build the Jewish state. Even Arab neighbors are important for the advance of the Labor movement and for long-range peace in the Middle East. The image of Acre will improve as its renowned history is appreciated by its residents and by visitors from overseas. The city offers opportunities to those who would work through its many groups and institutions for mutual benefit. The decision to remain in Acre or to move to a more westernized environment is a personal one. But it is also influenced by European and Israeli interpretations of the desirability of life in a middle-class, suburban area over life in the mosaic of a development city comprised of immigrants and refugees.

Many European Jewish immigrants have objected to the Oriental and working-class atmosphere of Acre as unsuitable for the rearing of their children. The sabras, on the other hand, identify more with Israeli institutions than with the traditions of their parents. They reject the notion that European civilization is superior to the Zionist state. They take a pragmatic view of the ambience of the development city. The level of career expectations and training has advanced throughout Israel in response to military needs and talents available in its academic centers and among the population. Acre is conveniently located in the military-industrial-educational complex generated by the Haifa Technical Institute and the Haifa Bay area. Some residents have assessed their situation and have found it possible to live a satisfying family and social life in Acre, while enjoying the benefits for training and employment provided by the region. Municipal leaders have tried to attract young couples by providing apartments and by enhancing the recreational facilities along the seashore. But they have to contend with prejudices, especially of European Jews and middle-class strivers. The city appeals mainly to those who can appreciate the Oriental flavor.

5 / Sephardi-Oriental Jews from Muslim lands

Jewish immigrants from countries that were once under Muslim domination constitute nearly half the population of Acre. The Sephardim originated in Spain, where they flourished under benign Moorish rule during the Middle Ages. By the close of the fifteenth century, they were driven out of the country by its Catholic conquerors. Others were persecuted by the Inquisition, even though they became converts. The Sephardim spoke a Judaeo-Spanish dialect, the current version of which is called Ladino. They found refuge throughout the Mediterranean basin—in North Africa, Egypt, and Ottoman Turkish domains in the Balkans and in the Levant. The Sephardim adopted the cultures of the lands in which they settled and intermingled the culture of the Berbers or Turks or Arabs with their traditional customs. A few came to their ancient homeland, where they formed religious communities in Jerusalem and Hebron, in Safed and in Tiberias. Evidence that some Sephardim settled in the vicinity of Acre has been found in a cemetery at the village called Kufr Yasif.

The Oriental Jews come from ancient communities in Mesopotamia (Babylonia), Persia, Yemenite Arabia, and parts of India. They are called Mizrachi, meaning "Eastern." They speak the languages of their host countries and are even less influenced by westernization than the Sephardi Jews.

The leaders of the state of Israel have made great efforts to bring these people into the country, under the policy of Ingathering of the Exiles. They view these immigrants as somewhat primitive and in need of assimilation to modern western and technological values. For their part, the Oriental Jews and the Sephardim consider themselves "purer" than the European Jews, who dominate the institutions. They resent the secularization of their religious communities and the alterations of their kinship groups. They have organized to participate in the institutional power structure through political bargaining and sometimes more overt demonstrations of discontent.

Despite the fact that they have many elements of culture in common with the Arabs, the Sephardi-Oriental Jews disdain the Arabs and try to decrease their identity with them so as to integrate with the European Jews. They are highly insulted when Europeans contemptuously refer to them as "Arabs" when they fail to adhere to westernized ways. The immigrants quickly drop the Arabic language for Hebrew, which is readily learned by them. They take up westernized styles of dress and household furnishings. They would readily give up their traditional foods, but many veteran Israelis and the sabra (native born) generation appreciate them. Although Israelis value Middle Eastern styles in ornaments and the performing arts, young Sephardi-Orientals prefer western cinema, pop music, the motorcycle cult, and other westernized ways. Israeli leaders call the western veneer on a Middle Eastern base "levantinism." They would prefer the Jewish immigrants and the Arabs to internalize the processes of social democracy and technical know-how. They are concerned with finding ways of halting the alienation that has spread among both the Arab and the Sephardi-Oriental youth.

The Sephardi Jews living in Acre during the Turkish period numbered several hundred families. They had a small synagogue in the Old City and they engaged in crafts and trade, living much as the Christian Arabs, who were also among the minorities. These Jews of Acre maintained contact with other Sephardi Jews who lived in the holy cities, some Galilean villages, and occasionally the larger centers under Ottoman rule. The city of Acre was in decline by the time the British took over the government of Palestine in 1918 and the Jewish community at that time was not notable. Zionist development of Haifa and the agricultural valleys influenced Acre's Jewish minority adversely, and when Arab nationalism erupted in riots throughout the country, the Jews of Acre abandoned the area by the end of the 1930s.

There is a large family living in Acre's New City, which is the remnant of Acre's Sephardi community from the time of Turkish rule. They are engaged now in extensive business enterprises. When the family was displaced through the riots between Arab and Jewish nationalists (on the eve of World War II), they found ready employment in the Haifa Bay area. The young men were attracted to Jewish military groups. Some cooperated in the Allied effort to halt German threats to the Middle East and the Jews of Palestine. Others joined terrorist organizations dedicated to ridding their homeland of British controls and the impact of the British White Paper, which denied refuge to the Jews of Europe. All members of the family were joyful at the establishment of Israel in 1948 and they participated in the liberation of Arab strongholds like Acre.

The family returned to its native city, but not to the Old City, which was now crowded with Arab and Jewish refugees and immigrants. In the Mandate New City, near the seashore, was a large villa where a Muslim and a Christian Arab family occupied the upper story. The Sephardi family gained title to the ground floor of the villa and much of its garden, which was filled with flowering shrubs and had a fountain in its center. The neighbors were friendly and observed the proprieties of their common Oriental culture, which had been strongly influenced by the modernizing tendencies of the British Mandate and now Israel.

The Sephardi family increased its resources by obtaining a franchise for gasoline and auto repair stations. Its status was further enhanced by a marriage between an older daughter and the son of the Ashkenazi Mayor, Gadish, who was an important figure in the development of Acre and the integration of its diverse people. The first television antenna on a rooftop in Acre was at the villa. The families were some of the first to watch the early programs in Arabic that came from Beirut. Hebrew television service was instituted a decade later (at which time both Oriental and western Jews were ready for it). The family's children returned to their home and entered the business after military service and the merchant marine. Their life style is a combination of hard work, moderate living, and satisfying social compensations.

A wedding celebration called forth extraordinary efforts on the part of the family, which revealed their traditional orientations and their status. An older son was married to a local girl who came from a Rumanian immigrant family. Sephardi kinsmen came from great distances to stay for several days at the villa and to party into the night. There was Oriental-style feasting and music together with newer Israeli motifs. The wedding, itself, took place at a tourist cafe at the seaside nearby. The ceremony was traditional and brief, but the reception was lavishly catered. Several hundred friends and neighbors, including the leaders of all ethnic communities in Acre, participated with exuberance.

This native Sephardi family had gained renown in Acre, which demonstrates the potential of Oriental Jews to become a bridge between the Ashkenazim and the Arabs. But the family is somewhat marginal in terms of the major institutions of the city. For example, it attends "Reform" religious services that are held in a neighborhood school during the high holy days. Men, women, and children sit together and pray in Hebrew and Ladino, unlike the Orthodox practice that separates men from women and does not use the secular language at all. The sponsors of these innovative services are Sephardim from Bulgaria. They have attracted Turkish and Egyptian Jews who prefer a "modern" congregation to the several traditional synagogues located in immigrant neighborhoods. The veteran family has avoided taking public political stands though its position might appear to warrant this. It focuses on having its business licenses renewed so that its enterprises might expand. The generation born in Israel attends local schools and makes friends there. The youths show no outstanding scholarly attainments; rather they prefer to assimilate into the emerging sabra meld of Acre, which is at ease with its environment. Thus the family is involved in the development process and accommodates to the changes that affect the city.

ORIENTAL COMMUNALISM IN TRANSITION

The largest Sephardi group in Acre and in Israel comes from North Africa, particularly Morocco, with smaller communities from Tunisia and Algeria. The Arabic name for this region is the Maghrib. It refers to those countries of the western Mediterranean where, during the early Middle Ages, Muslim Arab culture was superimposed on native Berber culture. The French conquered and colonized the coastal areas during the nineteenth century, and they brought their civilization and protection to minorities in the cities. The Jews of North Africa lived both in the countryside and in the city ghettos. They were a religious minority who feared the Muslim majority, but who benefited wherever French influence was strong. Overseas Jewish philanthropists subsidized their general education in Alliance Israelite Universelle schools and they received vocational training through the Organization for Rehabilitation through Training (O.R.T.). Family and community life were important among all classes and their religious beliefs gave them a messianic feeling about the Jewish Homeland in Palestine. A large-scale migration followed after the persecution of Jews by the Vichy French during World War II and also later, when Arab nationalist hostility mounted in the wake of the 1948 Arab-Israeli War. The World Zionist Organization sent emissaries to alert these North African Jews to their danger and to prepare them to leave for the new State of Israel.

The North African Jewish influx hit Israel during the period of postwar austerity when the institutions of the new state were strained and when bureaucratic norms often superseded Zionist values. The migrants spoke Arabic for the most part, their clothing was Oriental, and their skills were limited to shopkeeping and crafts. They became targets for the frustrations of European Jewish refugees with whom the bureaucrats could more easily identify and empathize. Even Israel's Arabs used the "Moroccans" as a reference point to deflect their hostilities to the very existence of the Jewish state and its policy of Ingathering the Exiles. The stereotype was widely spread through a film, "Sallah Shabtai," which depicted a wily immigrant family whose head managed to avoid hard work and entrapment by the government bureaucrats. For their part, the North African Jews considered themselves to be direct descendants of the Jews of the Roman Empire and the Judaeo-Arabic civilization that flourished in Spain during the Middle Ages. They felt that their religious and nationalist zeal was stronger than that of the Europeans because of their family and community loyalties. They wished their children to become sabras in Israel, living together with the Ashkenazi Jews of Europe, but they did not wish them to foresake all the customs of their ancestors.

A produce dealer from the Moroccan-Algerian border exemplifies the transition of the North African Jews from tribal and ghetto ways to full participation in the life of the development city of Acre. As he approaches middle age, he recalls the fear and hatred of the Arabs in his native land and his longing to celebrate the ritual of Passover in Israel. He remembers the Zionist emissaries who gathered families from many communities together and shipped them to reception centers outside the great French port of Marseilles. He remembers being bewildered at the complexity of paper work required to board a small Israeli vessel and marveling at the Jewish sailors in the crew. The Mediterranean voyage produced the miseries of seasickness for many families but, on deck, the youth (organized by Israeli leaders) danced the *hora* and sang the songs of pioneers in the Jewish Homeland. They landed at Haifa's docks where the elders kissed the holy ground and danced holding their Torah scrolls, which they had brought back "home" from "2000 years of Exile."

The absorption process in Israel brought disappointments as well as new experiences to the produce dealer and his kinsmen. They were shocked by the secular ways of the European Jewish bureaucrats who smoked on the Sabbath and who sat bareheaded at mealtime in the reception center. Religious party personnel seemed to be more observant, but they did not understand the customs of the North African immigrants. Passover was celebrated, but nobody brought lambs to the camp for the traditional sacrifice. Then communities were dispersed throughout the country in order to encourage assimilation and to fulfill security and agricultural needs for the fledgling nation. Young men were inducted into the army. The children were prepared for kindergartens and primary schools in Hebrew. The wives remained home to cook and to market in an atmosphere of perennial shortages and confusion. Labor exchanges assigned the men to physically demanding work projects of land reclamation and construction, for which they were unprepared.

The produce dealer and his family were directed to Acre to help maintain security there and because housing and employment seemed to be available. The move attracted other members of his clan, and they settled in abandoned Arab apartments in the New City just outside the walls. They avoided direct contact with Arabs in domestic life, but they did interact with them in the marketplace in the Old City. They found their Yiddish- and Rumanian-speaking Jewish neighbors another challenge. These were brethren with whom one was supposed to build a Homeland, but they were quarrelsome and insulting. Such experiences reinforced the importance of the traditional clan in providing fellowship and eventually political leverage in the absorption process.

An early experience showed the North Africans that they could manipulate the rivalries among the Labor and the Religious parties toward their own ends. There was an abandoned Arab store that the Labor-dominated Municipality authorized as a clubhouse for their political party. The North Africans were seeking several places for communal synagogues, so that they would not have to use their already overcrowded apartments. They demonstrated in front of the abandoned store, claiming that secularist Europeans were receiving preferential treatment over religious immigrants from the East. They were arrested by the police, since their presence at the store was illegal. The matter was finally resolved in their favor when Religious party leaders intervened in the Municipality where they were in the coalition with Labor. This made the North Africans loyal to the Religious party and it chastened Labor. Henceforth, the Labor groups went to great efforts to provide religious centers and to celebrate religious festivals in Oriental immigrant neighborhoods. North Africans joined Labor parties when they were able to provide the types of work and housing they could not get from the Religious parties. They were also sympathetic toward the Nationalists who were anti-Arab and opposed the domination of the veteran Labor hierarchy.

The life style of the produce dealer and his family was influenced by his ability to continue traditional community ties in an environment where national institutions determined many of life's options. Following a brief military service, the produce dealer obtained a license to open a small store, because his health was not strong enough for road work. He enjoyed his neighborhood because it was a mixture of family members and also European Jews who were civil servants and laborers. His hours of work were from dawn until dusk, but he took off several hours at midday to return to his home for traditional dinner and relaxation. He attended morning and evening prayer services at his communal synagogue nearby. The elders would gather at the shop to discuss religious affairs, finances, political allegiances, and personal matters. The greengrocer also managed to participate in the celebrations of his fellow congregants and the neighbors, including several that took place in midafternoon. His wife or children would substitute at the store, though they were not as adept at communicating with the customers. For the produce dealer, his communal role was more important than a flourishing business. Within his family, the children remained respectful even though they were becoming more secular through school and employment activities.

The produce dealer is proud of his children's achievements and the opportunities they have been given and, in turn, their contribution to the building of the Jewish Homeland. One son has become a skilled worker and he is active in labor union affairs. He has married a Sephardi girl and they live in a new neighborhood whose housing was subsidized by Labor movement and government funds. Another son married a Rumanian Jewish girl. Her family objected to the ethnic mix, but she preferred the warmth of the Sephardi family life. The produce dealer sponsored a modern wedding in a New City cafe with invitations going mainly to young friends of the couple. The older generation was received in the synagogue and at home in traditional fashion. The son has a civil service position in Haifa, which he obtained after military service. He has chosen to reside in Acre, where he has a new apartment and can enjoy the company of friends from school days. His parents dote on their blond granddaughter and the women of the household exchange traditional Moroccan and Israeli recipes.

Hebrew is now the language of the family except between the produce dealer and his wife and among the elders for whom Arabic still dominates. Younger sons and daughters prefer secular school and neighborhood activities to traditional communal and religious affairs, except during festivals. They anticipate military service and technical training. These changes will assure satisfying lives for them almost anywhere in the Jewish state.

SECULARIZING TENDENCIES

In many Sephardi families there is a more radical separation from traditional culture to the Oriental environment represented in Acre. There is a two-generation family consisting of brothers who came to Israel from Casablanca where they had been exposed to French and to American military personnel during World War II. They learned to value western material culture and mechanical skills. They sought relief from Arab nationalist oppression in Morocco and they felt that they would prosper in a Jewish Homeland. They left behind most of their traditional practices and identified with the Labor Zionist movement. They joined the more leftist party, MAPAM, because there seemed to be greater opportunity of challenging the monopoly of Europeans in the Labor Federation and the Municipality. They were willing to tolerate MAPAM's philosophy of integrating Israel's Arabs and Jews, despite their strong prejudices against the Arabs. Occasionally, they supported the Nationalists, but they did not affiliate with them publicly.

One brother learned Hebrew rapidly and qualified as a postal worker following his military service. He had a secure position and friendships among the Sephardim who dominated Acre's postal service association. He secured a loan for an apartment in the expanding center of Acre's New City. The furnishings are modern and neighbors are of appropriate status. His children have graduated from secondary school and one son has become an engineer through courses at Haifa's Technical Institute. There appears to be flexibility in the family relationships so that the younger generation feels equally free to remain in Acre or leave it for professional opportunities elsewhere.

The other brother has been slower to accommodate to life in the development city. In order to avoid living in the Old City among the Arabs, the family obtained a small Arab-style apartment in a transitional neighborhood in the New City. The father was a welder who earned a good salary, but he preferred to save his money and to pay for new housing without loans. Meanwhile, his family grew to five children and their apartment became intolerably crowded. The wife was status-conscious, speaking French rather than Arabic until her Hebrew improved. The children joined Marxist MAPAM youth clubs and visited nearby kibbutzim for recreation and for ideological indoctrination. The mother was disturbed that her oldest son might become what she considered to be a "peasant" on a kibbutz rather than a physical education teacher. She was pleased when her daughter left the kibbutz to take secretarial courses. The children seemed to desire to escape from the household, since they were embarrassed by traditional practices, such as their father lounging in pajamas on the Sabbath.

The middle son, who was only a fair student but likeable, faced a personal crisis at the time of his *bar mitzvah* (coming of age). The event was delayed until the family could move into its new apartment and hold a modern reception. But construction was not completed and the family's finances were not as far along as the father wished. It was simple enough to attend a weekday religious service in a communal synagogue for the bar mitzvah, but the reception had to be held in the small apartment. Only the family was invited and a homemade chicken dinner with Oriental vegetables was served on the balcony just above the unpaved street. The cousins danced outside to phonograph and accordion music, but the neighbors did not join in. As night fell, the adults moved inside to the main room where the music alternated between Mediterranean tango and Moroccan Arabic. As the brandy took effect, the men paired off to do Oriental-style dancing. This both amused and embarrassed the ladies and the younger generation. The party was a success although more limited than the status-conscious family wished.

The father finally vindicated his status by moving into a new and ample apartment in the city's center. In order to help pay for the Danish-style furniture, the mother went to work in a canning factory. This did not seem to affect her status concerns since it was for highly focused goals. The family made new friends among the neighbors and even began to speak well of young Arab families who were participating in an experiment in integrated housing here. The younger children continued their schooling and they enjoyed the company of their schoolmates. They were preparing to leave Acre for life styles they felt were more in the spirit of modern Israel. The family perceived Acre as a transitional community that enabled them to break from tradition and to learn how to make a new life in the Jewish Homeland.

BRIDGE VERSUS MARGINALITY

Several conditions facilitate the Sephardim in providing a bridge between European Jews and local Arabs. Many Jews from Syria, Egypt, Tunisia, and Algeria have been exposed to French and British education. They have qualified for positions in the Israeli government and Acre municipal service institutions and the Labor Federation after participating in intensive Hebrew and administrative training courses. Friendships among these young Sephardi officials have formed in the postal services, the banks, among grammar school teachers, and other occupational groupings. They provide each other with information about qualifying for better positions that lead to a middle-class life style in neighborhoods with new apartments. In public, the young Sephardim can communicate equally well with Arabs and with European Jews. They must cope with hostility that stems from rivalries as they take over jobs the Arabs feel they should have and which pressure the Europeans who now feel outnumbered. Daily interaction with the diverse ethnic groups aims at being "correct." Relationships between colleagues are incorporated into the family celebrations to which wide circles are invited. Common interests develop through political party coalitions, thus meeting both personal and group objectives.

Sephardi Jews have succeeded to Labor Federation leadership positions in Acre during the past decade. They became active in heavy industrial unions and led the strikes. This especially threatened national Labor Federation and Labor party leaders, because the heavy industry was sponsored by a conglomerate of government, Labor movement, and private capital to further the development of the country and the local region. In some instances the Labor Federation had strike leaders pensioned off and co-opted into the local branch. This was perceived as prestigious by the individual worker and his ethnic group as it became a stepping-stone to further office-holding.

The strength of the Sephardim has been limited by pervasive factionalism. Traditionally religious and modern secular groups are at odds. There are rivalries among the different clans and groups from different regions of North Africa as well as between them and the more westernized urban Jews from Egypt, Syria, and Iraq. When a Middle Eastern Jew was elected mayor of Acre during the late 1960s, it was thought that he would provide a focus of integration for all Jewish and Arab groups, since he was conversant with them and had considerable administrative experience. But the North Africans manipulated Labor's rivalry with the Nationalists in order to gain support for one of their own aspirants. The Europeans continued to control the selection process, though they could not unite on a candidate from their own ranks until the city's very viability was threatened. Outside party pressure forced them to support an Ashkenazi Labor Federation official from a minority party for succeeding elections. Meanwhile, the North Africans expected to win the highest offices in the city because their youth had gained prestige from their participation in the 1967 War and their numbers were great.

Advances in assimilation and integration are made by Sephardim who are active in the commercial and professional life of the city. The Bulgarians have been outstandingly successful in communicating with Ashkenazi Rumanians and with Sephardi Turks and Egyptians, who, in turn, serve as a bridge to the North Africans. During Nazi occupation of their country, the Bulgarian monarch protected the Jewish minority from deportation. Many were able to migrate to Israel with capital resources before the Communist takeover. Several modern stores along Ben Ami Street in Acre's New City are operated by Bulgarian Jews. Others contribute to the city's supply of physicians and health-care personnel, bank clerks, and city officials. They are involved more in civic life than in politics. They have drawn other Sephardic groups together through the Reform services for the high holy days. They may intermarry with Ashkenazi Jews according to social class and similar interests.

Acre's Turkish Jews have more sizable numbers than the Bulgarians and they are in a variety of occupations. They were threatened by Nazi influence in Turkey during World War II and they hastened to migrate to Israel to prevent becoming a persecuted minority like the Greeks. The entrepreneurs with greater capital settled in the major cities of Israel, some having connections there since the British Mandate and Ottoman periods at the time of World War I. In cities like Acre, the Turkish Jews are small shopkeepers but many were forced to take factory jobs because the economy could not support many tradesmen. The Turkish Jews have a community synagogue in the eastern immigrant quarter and they participate in both Labor and Religious party life. In some enterprising families, the wives have helped their husbands to carry on business from pushcarts. They have used political means and emphasized physical handicaps to acquire licenses for shops in Acre's Old City. The ultimate achievement is to open a shop on the main street of the New City and to achieve recognition in synagogue and political circles. Turkish Jews feel able to communicate with Arabic-speaking as well as Ladino-speaking communities, and they do not feel distant from Balkan groups such as the Bulgarians and Rumanians. The Israeli generation is assimilating rapidly to secular and technical skills through the schools, youth movements, and military service. They may marry either Sephardim or Ashkenazim, depending on social class and the strength of traditional community and family ties.

Acre's Egyptian Jews form a viable bridge between Sephardi and Ashkenazi communities as well as to the Arabs. Many have had English and French education, and have been exposed to modern urban Arab culture in Egypt. Upon learning Hebrew they have been able to transfer their skills to a variety of professions, including engineering, accounting, medicine, and general administrative work. Many Egyptian Jews, who were able to bring capital out of the country, have opened shops in the Old and the New Cities of Acre. There are large numbers who became workers and members of the Labor Federation during the austerity period, when tradesmen could not be absorbed. They have worked themselves into all positions in the political and Labor hierarchy. Traditionalists live in the immigrant quarter where they have a synagogue. Mobile families mingle with middle-class peers from diverse backgrounds.

Feelings of marginality prevail among Sephardi-Oriental groups who are unable to use leverage in institutional coalitions. In Acre, there is a minority group called the Karaites, who consider themselves to be purer than even the Orthodox Jewish establishment. They remain outside the Jewish fold because their ancestors never accepted rabbinical teachings that emerged among other Jewish communities following the dispersion of the Jews under Roman rule. The Karaites come from Egyptian cities where they were entrepreneurs and government officials. They fled to Israel as refugees following persecution during the Arab-Israeli War of 1948 and the Sinai Campaign of 1956. Since they were educated in Middle Eastern and European languages and skills, they attained office jobs in Israel. Their success as entrepreneurs was limited by the amount of capital they could smuggle out of the country through European or North American third parties.

The Karaite community in Acre, which consists of a few dozen families, is half a day's journey from its center in Ramle. It meets in private homes for Sabbath services and for social life. The Karaites have kept away from established Religious party schools or political affiliation because of discrimination against them. Marriage between a Jew and a Karaite would be considered a mixed marriage and hence forbidden by the rabbinate. Those Karaites who accommodate to Acre society find their way to secular Labor groups. Large numbers have preferred to migrate to France or to French Canada to join kinsmen who had acquired passports during previous generations when France protected minorities in the old Turkish Empire. The generation that grows up and remains in Acre is exposed to the secular Hebrew schools. It is likely to assimilate to technical culture and may try to amalgamate with other Jewish groups through marriage, perhaps undergoing formal Orthodox Jewish "conversion" to do so.

Jews from Middle Eastern countries further removed from the Mediterranean have had severe problems of marginality in Israel and in Acre. The size of the ethnic migrant community and its ability to make contact with other Jews and with Arabs affect the direction of the marginality and its resolution. Jews from Iraq came to Israel early during the 1950s on a rescue airlift. Many brought a somewhat urbanized culture which had been influenced by British and other western institutions between the two world wars. The Iraqi Jews considered themselves to be the direct descendants of the Jews of ancient Babylonia. They felt their minority status would end when they joined their coreligionists in the Jewish Homeland. The hundred thousand migrants were dispersed to development villages and towns where they found themselves in competition with Ashkenazi and Sephardi immigrants for services and status. They gained their way by influencing political parties and government institutions. However, they lacked the effectiveness of the Egyptian Jews who, through their historical proximity to Turkish and British Mandate Palestine, could mediate between Ashkenazi and Sephardi communities.

The small size of the Iraqi-Jewish group in Acre limits its viability as a community. Individual Iraqi Jews with appropriate education or professional certification have been drawn into government work, especially into education for Arabic-speaking youth. Unfortunately those who were assigned to Arab schools during a period of teacher-shortage and security concerns gained the animosity of Muslim and Christian leaders, despite their conscientious attempts to perform well. The Iraqi Jews also found Acre too distant from their ethnic centers in the Tel Aviv area and the Southern District of the country. The group has departed from Acre in order to seek a combination of traditional community support and further opportunities in larger places.

Jews from Iran form a remnant of the ancient Persian community. In Acre they are marginal because of the small size of the group and the fact that its local residents are semiskilled and not very familiar with modern ways. There is no social relationship with the prestigious Bahai or with Arabs or Mediterranean or European Jews. In the absorption process, the men and youths have joined labor exchanges and labor unions. They are catered to by Religious and Labor parties, but they do not supply active candidates for office. The new generation benefits from public schooling and the military service. But family ties have been broken by the policy of ethnic dispersion and by generational differences in orientation toward secular life in Israel. Persian Jewish life in Israel continues in isolated village settlements or in the quarters of large cities like Jerusalem. In Acre the group seems to be in a double minority status.

The Yemenite Jews come from a background in Arabia that is even more isolated and traditional than the Jews from Iran or other countries of central Asia. They have benefited from their image as hard workers in agriculture, which Israelis admire over the urban unskilled tasks to which other Middle Eastern Jews have gravitated. The Yemenite Jewish community in Acre is small but cohesive, and it works in the forestation projects of the Jewish National Fund, a society greatly admired by Zionist ideologists. Membership in the Labor Federation has acquainted the Yemenites with the strike as a powerful weapon for better conditions, and it has taught them about the advantages of cohesiveness for political action. In Israel, immigrant Yemenite wives work outside the home because their husbands are often too old to support the family. Their freedom has increased as they have left domestic service for work in industry where their diligence is highly regarded. The Israeli-born daughters extend this liberation through secular education and military service. In Acre the valedictorian of the evening Hebrew class conducted by the Municipality was a Yemenite wife and mother. A young man became a favorite teacher in the religious schools and a leader in the integrated chapel services. Israeli secularism has destroyed many Yemenite family values, but the women and youths have been eager to take on the new ways and to become absorbed quickly.

THE "OTHER" ISRAEL AND NEW REFERENCE GROUPS

Large numbers of Sephardi-Oriental Jews have found it so difficult to accommodate to westernized Zionist goals that it has given them a negative image in the country and the towns where they predominate. They constitute the "other" Israel. While their employment, school attendance, political activity, and participation in the nation's defense efforts show marked improvement each year and over the decades, the gap between Middle Eastern and European Jews remains wide. The Sephardi-Oriental Jews have emulated westernized ways and they have cast off much of their Arabic heritage, but in the process a great alienation has affected both elders and youth. Traditional patriarchy in family and community life and customs based on religious practices and identification with the clan have broken down. It has been possible for workers and officials and their children to participate in locally based national institutions such as the Labor Federation, political parties, youth movements, and the schools where there is an incentive to intermingle with Jews from other countries. But the models and the norms have been derived from the European-based history of the Zionist movement and pioneering in the Jewish Homeland. Government reports show that the highest rates of unemployment, delinquency, overcrowded housing, and neighborhood disturbance occur in districts inhabited by Jewish immigrants from Middle Eastern countries. It is surmised that traditional values are no longer providing the people with gratification from their citizenship in the Jewish Homeland. Their hostility has been deflected against neighboring Arabs as illustrated by incidents in Acre during 1961, 1965, and 1969. More recently, a "Black Panther" group emerged in the slums of Jerusalem criticizing the Labor and social democratic institutions of the national government. These Oriental Jews have drawn support from small groups aligned with international New Left movements, and this has brought them some notoriety and much criticism from the leaders of all Zionist parties.

In Acre there is great awareness both among institutional officials and the more veteran European settlers that Sephardi-Oriental youth in particular must be given a feeling of involvement in the history and destiny of the city and the nation. The Municipal Department of Education sponsors day camps during the summer which attract both Jewish and Arab youth. Leadership is recruited from among teachers and youths from secondary school. The programs include story-telling in Arabic for Arab children and in Hebrew for European and Middle Eastern Jewish children, following the pattern of schooling. The Oriental Jewish children are thus drawn to their brethren from the West (which is government policy). Athletics and crafts mingle all the children according to age group, and there is a conscious effort to prevent rivalry based on ethnicity per se. In the long run, the children tend to affiliate with schoolmates from their own neighborhood so that this becomes the basis for most affirmative interaction.

A more militant example of Sephardi-Oriental identification with Israel and its separation from Arabic influence is provided by a day camp sponsored by the delinquency prevention section of the local police. Mature and responsive Arab and Jewish counselors planned their activities in a coordinated fashion and even socialized after the camp period was over, which is a sign of developing friendliness. The divisions between Arabs and Jews were reemphasized, however, by the selection of themes each side chose to represent them for the duration of the camp period. Following their leader's suggestion, the Arab youth promoted the symbol of the United Nations and its peace-keeping mission. The Jewish youth, with the passive acquiescence of their counselors, adopted the Israeli Defense Forces as their theme. The Arab youth developed emblems of the countries of the world, without overemphasis on Middle Eastern states. The Jewish youth collected the insignia of famous Israeli regiments and they gleefully participated in the raising and lowering of the national flag, whose emblem is derived from the Zionist movement and the six-pointed star of David. Arab-Jewish intergroup relations were not notably advanced by this experience.

Because the political structure of Israel and Acre favors the Labor and the Religious parties, most Middle Eastern Jews support the coalition in hopes of achieving appropriate benefit and recognition. While this has indeed occurred as a result of numbers, demonstrations, and other forms of leverage, large groups of alienated Sephardic-Orientals have sought favors from the opposition parties. The Nationalist Likud party has attracted many because it accuses the Labor Federation of being a monopoly of veteran and European Jews. It also has a strong anti-Arab policy that appeals to emigrants from Middle Eastern countries though in actuality the leadership within this party is also dominated by westerners. But there has been a conscious effort to show how Sephardi Jews from the days of the British Mandate in Palestine actively participated in the violence that caused the British to leave and the Arabs to fear the Jews. Acre is brought into the history through a Museum to Heroes and Martyrs, which occupies part of the former British prison in the old Turkish citadel. Streets surrounding this site have had their names changed to commemorate Sephardi-Oriental members of the Irgun Zvei Leumi, the extremist military group. The Labor and Religious coalition has agreed to the changes in order to provide new reference groups for Acre's Oriental Jewish citizens. The coalition feels it can combat Sephardi-Oriental alienation and its attraction toward the right-wing opposition by a show of national unity.

An unpaved street called "Mediterranean" was the scene of a name-changing ceremony on a late summer afternoon during the fieldwork period. Municipal workers installed flag poles and the Zionist-Israeli national emblem was unfurled. This occurred in a neighborhood just outside the prison walls, which also contained Moroccan immigrant houses and the government school for Arabs (closed during this season). Early participants included officials from the Mayor's Office, the Planning and Engineering Department, the Labor Federation, and the Police. They were all active in the Labor coalition. They were also all Sephardim, from Egypt, Syria, and North Africa. The local youth drum and bugle corps performed under the auspices of the Municipal Department of Recreation. The Mayor, who was a veteran of the Russian-Polish front against the Nazis, a school administrator, and a Labor party leader, welcomed the guests, who were eastern European veterans of the Jewish underground in Palestine and now officials in the Nationalist party. The invocation was given by an Ashkenazi rabbi, who had assisted the prisoners in the notorious fortress. They had been hanged for assassinating a British government official in Cairo in 1943 in revenge for the White Paper which forbade Jewish immigration into the country from Nazi-dominated Europe. The street was renamed "Two Eliahus" after the hero-martyrs, and it was emphasized that these were Palestinian Jews whose ancestors had lived in the Mediterranean region throughout its history. The rivalries between Labor and the Nationalists and the Jews from west and east were to be resolved through renewed efforts toward building a Jewish Homeland together. As the sun set the assembly began the Jewish prayer service, which linked together secularists and traditionalists from many lands.

The integration of Middle Eastern and European Jews has been achieved at the expense of the Arabs, or perhaps it has been catalyzed by the Arab presence. Government policy of Hebrew language study in Jewish schools and other institutions has caused a decline in the use of Arabic among the Oriental Jews and has accelerated their accommodation to Zionist programs. Compulsory military service for all Jewish young men and for young women who are not from strictly Orthodox homes is a means of influencing immigrants who might lack formal schooling. They are taught basic literacy and they can learn trades while in the military service. Their military experience focuses their hostility against the Arab enemies of the country. Participation in the war makes them heroes within their families and in their neighborhoods. They know they will receive full recognition if they die in battle or in border clashes, and will be memorialized along with generations of patriots in the ceremony preceding Israel's Independence Day. Because of a numerical majority, the Oriental Jewish communities in Acre have provided a high proportion of black-bordered portraits gathered in government-sponsored books honoring the war dead.

The violence that accompanies local Arab and Sephardi-Oriental relations interferes with the image of the city of Acre as a model for appropriate majority-minority interaction. The incidents involving Terra Sancta Arab youth demonstrations in 1961 and the Arab terrorists in 1969 have already been described. The local Arab has earned the mistrust of the Jews not without cause, and the Oriental Jewish reputation for aggressiveness and hostility has been reinforced. An episode in the summer of 1965 contributed to Arab-Jewish division while at the same time it enhanced Sephardi-Oriental identification with heroes in Israel. An immigrant Jew from Egypt named Eli Cohen went to Damascus in Syria where he passed himself off as an Arab military expert and gained the confidence of the leadership there. Somebody recognized his photograph in a local newspaper and he was arrested as an Israeli spy. He was hanged and the Syrians refused to return the body to his family across the border. This was a great dishonor and was taken as an indication that he had been tortured and perhaps mutilated. On the thirtieth day after his death, which is an intensive period of mourning in Jewish religious tradition, youth groups from Israel's military program organized a relay race from the Syrian border in the north to the Cohen family home south of Tel Aviv. The runners were scheduled to halt in Acre at dusk and a large assembly of local groups was planned at the soldiers' memorial marker for the War of Independence of 1948. Youths and adults from all political parties and military contingents cheered the runners as their torches came in sight. The mayor and a military officer exaulted the heroism of Eli Cohen as an example to the youth of Israel and they referred to his Sephardic origins as a source of pride to the immigrants from Arab lands. Poems of bravery and dedication followed as the crowd remained very quiet, with an air of tenseness. A scuffle broke out, but it was quickly controlled by the police. As the ceremony ended, the youth groups dispersed down the roads to waiting buses that would take them to nearby kibbutzim and the suburbs of Haifa. Local youths marched toward the seashore and the citadel on the edge of the Old City.

A week later at a meeting between Jewish youth leaders and the police on matters relating to the responsibilities of citizenship and domestic tranquility, it was admitted that an incident had taken place the night of Eli Cohen's memorial. Arab youths were rumored to have made remarks approving the action of the Syrians and later on they had been beaten up on the main street of the New City. Adults present at the memorial service had noticed a false calm that anticipated a suggestion to march on Arab quarters. This did not happen, but journalists came to the scene and exploited the incident.

The adverse newspaper publicity exposed the Jews of Acre, particularly the Sephardi-Orientals, as hostile toward the Arabs and a threat to Israel's goals for an integrated majority-minority population. The mayor was accused of being unable to control the situation and the public was reminded of previous mistakes by the city's officials. Jewish and Arab leaders were quick to praise the efforts of the police to control outbreaks, but they blamed local political figures for general ineptitude and insensitivity. The Muslim religious judge proclaimed that he would lead the Arabs out of Acre into Lebanon if the authorities could not control the youth. Until tensions calmed down, the dedication of a marker memorializing Eli Cohen, scheduled for the public garden alongside the Municipality, was delayed for many months.

Such incidents as these Arab-Jewish outbreaks involving Sephardi-Oriental youths are not unique to Acre. That same summer, Yemenite Jews in Tel Aviv-Jaffa and Iraqi Jews in Ramle beat up local Arabs. As election time approached during the fall of 1965, the political candidates vied with one another to condemn the situation that led to the existence of the "Other" Israel and warned of the adverse international ramifications attendant on Arab-Jewish friction. They feared alienation as a political force, if the institutions of the state could not absorb Sephardi-Oriental youth. However, they defended Israel's security program and they urged local and neighboring Arabs to make peace.

The amalgamation of Sephardi-Oriental Jews in Acre and in Israel is proceeding rapidly despite the problems of intergroup relations, status, and alienation. Peer group, occupational, and political party associations are replacing traditional forms of ethnic community identity. Marriages between Sephardi-Oriental and Ashkenazi Jews have increased. Military service exposes youth to national perspectives and many veterans seek new neighborhoods away from their parents and ethnic communities. Acre still appeals to large numbers because of employment opportunities in industry and in office work and the professions. The Municipality is supporting the integration of its Israeli-born generation by appeals to national agencies for more housing and employment. A local policy gives preference to local citizens in official hiring. For the Sephardi-Orientals, life in Acre provides a transition from the villages and ghettos of the Middle Eastern countries of their origin. The New City is separated from the main Arab quarter, but it is accessible if one wishes an Oriental atmosphere. A desirable style of life is provided by the presence of family and friends, convenient services, and the pleasant atmosphere of the seashore. It is possible to know the city's leaders and to participate in community activities that link the development city to national societal objectives.

6 / Daily life and normative roles

The following description of life in Acre is a composite drawn from fieldwork. It illustrates family life, the world of work, and the youth culture. The pace of life varies with the time of day, the days of the week, and the changing seasons of the year. Israeli life styles are emerging through a synthesis of dominant European Jewish influences and Middle Eastern Jewish and Arab contributions, which are mediated and directed by Zionist ideology. At present, daily life in Acre functions within the development policy of the State of Israel. When the people's behavior accords with these goals and they act in the light of their personal needs and backgrounds, they are fulfilling normative roles in a local setting.

EARLY MORNING

At sunrise the *muezzin* traditionally climbs the minaret of the mosque to call the faithful to prayer. In Acre (as elsewhere), an amplified recording has replaced the voice of the sheikh who once performed this duty, since his recent death at a venerable age. At the Jazzar Mosque, the most imposing religious structure in the city, small coteries of men garbed in robes and traditional headgear enter the beautifully patterned courtyard made of colorful geometric tiles. Its garden is filled with flowering shrubs and small lemon trees and it is a place of tranquility and beauty. The men wash their feet and hands at a public fountain just outside the entrance. Within the mosque, they take prescribed positions of prayer on majestic oriental rugs covering the tile floor. Meanwhile in other quarters of the Old City, bells announce the mass in several Christian Arab churches. A few women come and light candles to their deceased family members. With the teachers from the Order of the Dames de Nazareth, they respond to the priestly blessings.

Clusters of Jewish men gather in distinctive Ashkenazi and Sephardi-Oriental synagogues at dawn in the New City's immigrant neighborhoods. They adjust their caps and put on prayer shawls, which have silver collar bands and stripes of black or blue. The men finger the woolen fringes of the ritual garment they are wearing, in whose ample folds they expect to be buried when their days are ended. During morning prayer service the men remove from velvet bags little black boxes with leather thongs called *tephillin*, or phylacteries. They place one on the forehead and wind the other around the left forearm according to instructions found in Deuteronomy (6:4-9). These sacred words are also enscrolled in ornate cases, called *mezuzoth*, which are fastened to the doorposts of houses and public buildings used by Jews. These prayers are fundamental to the Hebrew tradition and are introduced with the *Shma'*, which begins: "Hear, Oh Israel, the Lord is God, the Lord is One." It is recited several times during religious services. This is also the final invocation to the Almighty which a man must recite before his death. During the early morning hours, the religious practices form a background for the more mundane activities of the population.

Most people in Acre are not involved in religious services; rather, they arise to prepare themselves for work and for study. Families begin the day together, before they go their separate ways with other citizens occupied with similar pursuits. Family members rise at about six in the morning on workdays and preparations for breakfast take place amidst an atmosphere of haste. Rivkah, a conscientious housewife of Acre, awakes first and goes to the lavatory, which is next to the toilet, to splash water on her face and hands. She puts on a robe and fetches the kettle which she will put on the gas range to boil water for tea or coffee. She prepares a farina-like cereal with hot milk and sugar for her youngest child, Uri. Breakfast for herself and her husband, Shlomo, and their school-aged son, Danny, and daughter, Miriam, will consist of fresh hot rolls, eggs, and a vegetable salad. The radio is put on at full blast to awaken the sleepy ones and to catch the latest news about dramatic events on Israel's troubled borders. Rivkah is also in a hurry to strip the beds and to set the bedding out on the balcony to air. She must make sure her husband gets off to work and the children are on time for school with some nourishment for the active day ahead.

It is customary to send the children to the local grocery for fresh breakfast foods and lunch items. This is a carryover from austerity times, when supplies were limited and storage facilities consisted of an ice chest. Cooking was done on a kerosene burner then. Gradually, it has become possible to purchase food a day or two before hand and store it in the refrigerator, which also has a small freezer compartment. But the people prefer bread that is only a few hours out of the bakery and vegetables that have been delivered most recently to the produce dealer, located next to the grocery. The basic local menu includes Arab flat bread, called *pitta*, olives, white cheese, and *lebaniye* (yogurt), which are followed by hot tea with much sugar. More affluent and Europeanized families prefer white rolls or slices of white bread, spread with butter or margarine and served with fruit preserves or honey. The salad consists of green peppers, radishes, onions, tomatoes, and other raw vegetables in season. Ashkenazi men often add salt herring, thus making a hearty meal that is still moderate in price.

The grocer opens his store before dawn and is prepared for the stream of customers who are in a hurry to shout orders for breakfast and lunch supplies. They bring string bags and glass or plastic containers for refills. If food delivery is late, the schedules of an entire neighborhood are thrown out of line. Some youths and grownups still buy their lunch sandwiches of spiced meats, cheese, or smoked fish on the way to work or school. However, such last minute preparations are less frequent, since storage facilities both at home and in the stores have improved.

Seasonal fruits and vegetables may be purchased for morning snacks or lunches during this early trip, but the housewife will shop for her produce later when she goes to the market. Some milk is still delivered by wagon and boiled at home, but pasteurization and bottling are now prevalent. Most people heat the milk and drink it in cocoa or coffee or serve it with cereal rather than drinking it cold. Soft drinks and wines are purchased later in the day and are served at noontime and evening meals. Children or husbands help to carry bottles and to return the empty ones. Thus all members of the family participate in some way in the purchase of foodstuffs, though the main responsibility belongs to the mother, whose schedule is geared to this.

The radio in the morning provides something for everyone's taste. Local news and music is broadcast through the government station, Kol Yisrael (The Voice of Israel). Programming caters to diverse age and ethnic groups and is educational as well as entertaining. Hebrew language dominates, but Arabic and European languages are also heard. It is possible to extend one's exposure to diverse languages, political views, and music through readily accessible stations in neighbor-

Hebrew kindergarten graduation exercises.

ing countries in the Mediterranean and the Middle East, as well as outlets of the British Broadcasting Company (B.B.C.). The family pays special attention to the news, which sends their spirits high or low, depending on the state of war or peace. Weather reports send warnings of the desert wind, called the *sharav* or *hamsin*, in the summer and of rain and storms in the winter. The family is much concerned with news about sports events, particularly soccer, which is called "football," and all activities in which Israeli athletes may be competing with foreign stars. The outcome of Sabbath "football" games among local teams, sponsored by Labor or other political groups, leads to local pride or gloom. Musical programs bring traditional sacred services to all the ethnic and religious groups that desire them. Zionist "folk songs" of pioneer days are spirited and also nostalgic, though they bring smiles to contemporary youth. Discotheque numbers are in a subtle sabra dialect of Hebrew and they satirize current conditions in the country and the world. The cafe music of the Mediterranean and the Middle East is more romantic. Martial airs and speeches from neighboring Arab states seek to inspire their people to continue the struggle against Israel. Jews often wonder aloud if local Arabs will be affected by such programming which is constantly heard in the Old City cafes.

After breakfast the family members turn to their activities for the day. The children pack their books and lunches for school. The father rushes off to the bus that takes him to his factory. The mother is left to clear the dishes and to tend the baby. She must make plans for the family's return and for relaxation in the early evening.

OFF TO WORK

Husband Shlomo runs down the street toward the bus station. He is dressed in an open-necked shirt and wears slacks and shoes that once were used only on the Sabbath. He is hatless now, although formerly, when he was more religiously observant, he wore a cap or beret. He still does not eat meat and dairy products together. These days, however, he does not attend synagogue except during major festivals, but he does enjoy sacred music and considers the Sabbath the proper day for rest. He is more concerned with his survival in the material world. He joins his comrades at the newsstand where they select their national daily paper according to their favorite political philosophy. Most newspapers are sponsored by the parties and the few others take ideological positions relative to government policies. The men may choose a newspaper printed in Hebrew, Arabic, or some European idiom. They scan the international and national events that are reported on the front page. Then they turn to sports news and to local items on the inside pages. This enables them to fill in background that has already been covered by the radio news bulletins. There are sufficiently diverse points of view in the group to make extensive conversation during travel and at the factory.

The workers consider the bus ride to be a necessary part of the routine for getting to work. Motorcycle use has increased among young adults and bicycles are used for shorter distances. Administrators and minor officials use group taxis to travel between major cities, since passenger cars are still too expensive. Their ownership has increased, however, especially among white-collar and professional persons with means. The modern air-cooled bus is probably the optimum form of transportation, because it can take to side roads as well as the major arteries. The railroad service is limited to passengers who wish leisurely transportation to Haifa, Tel Aviv, and Jerusalem. The regular buses are less luxurious than those employed for tourism, but they are a great improvement over the venerable transport that the EGGED cooperative provided during the early days of Palestine's Jewish Community and during World War II.

Some passengers on the bus read their newspapers, but groups of workers usually socialize and catch up on interpersonal affairs. They greet one another with a hearty "Shalom," and inquire after families and health. Shlomo learns that one comrade is away for a month's military reserve training. All men take their turn in order to prepare the country for instant mobilization should an emergency be declared. The eventualities of war and the requirements for defense help explain why the people carry transistor radios with them and tune in to the hourly news bulletins. They learn about fallen neighbors and incidents involving attacks on civilians in public places. This makes people tense but also determined to resist.

Some of the conversation on Shlomo's bus turns to personal plans and celebrations. A young comrade has just purchased a new apartment and there will be a housewarming for all the friends on a Saturday night. Both husband and wife work and they saved for their apartment through Labor Federation accounts. They will have two bedrooms and a balcony in a newer section of the city. This is a long-awaited change from immigrant accommodations; yet, it is not too far away from old acquaintances. They are pleased that the children will attend a school where the other pupils are congenial. The family had thought of moving to Naharya because there is too much "trouble" in Acre among Arabs and Oriental Jews. But they concluded that only "snobs" move to the garden suburbs and there is opportunity in Acre, especially for workers' families, if the people become involved in local affairs.

Shlomo checks on rumors that the works committee at their factory is planning to call a strike. He knows that the cost of living has escalated and the workers resent the speedup instituted by management. They are especially bitter that their employers include the Labor Federation and kibbutz officials because the factory is owned jointly by government, Labor, and private interests. Management has warned the workers that production was interrupted by many wild-cat strikes last year and that the export quotas have not been met. They note that this causes a disservice to the state when foreign exchange is still imbalanced. Shlomo and his friends do not really like strike periods either, because tension is high and there are endless meetings and voting so that it is not really a vacation. The take-home pay is very small during a strike period, and then the family can't make bank deposits for the children's secondary school tuition. Shlomo and his comrades feel that the government should intervene to change the treatment of workers by the managers and to control inflation. He is thinking about changing his political affiliation to one of the minor parties within the Labor movement if matters do not improve.

Shlomo likes the routine of going to work each day with a friendly group of companions. He muses how each one has his own "personality" and would run the factory operation in his own way if he could. He extends these feelings to Jews in general, remarking that Jewish individualism has enabled the group to survive. He believes that Jews do get together and cooperate at times of crisis, as during the early days of the State of Israel. He prefers an active stance and he decries passivity. The lessons of the Nazi Holocaust of the Jews of Europe are often mentioned as a constant reminder that initiative is necessary for survival and for development.

Shlomo seeks to increase his material comforts although he knows he can live more simply if necessary. He criticizes Orientals who go into debt for ostentatious weddings and family celebrations. He feels a worker who earns a good income should invest it in improved housing, clothes, travel, and, above all, education for his children. He condemns such "luxuries" among his neighbors as holding *bar mitzvah* receptions in cafes and taking trips to Europe. He acknowledges that the government needs taxes and savings bonds in order to rescue more immigrants and to invest in the country's development. He is especially vehement about Israel's new "millionaires," who are creating elite groups just as in Europe. His ideal is a Workers' Commonwealth and he sees this carried out more through MAPAM's philosophy than through the dominant Labor party, MAPAI. Yet, he supports MAPAI because it contributed David Ben-Gurion, Moshe Sharett, and Golda Meir whom he believes have been the main creative forces of the Jewish Homeland. Yet Shlomo is caustic about the arrogance of Labor Federation officials

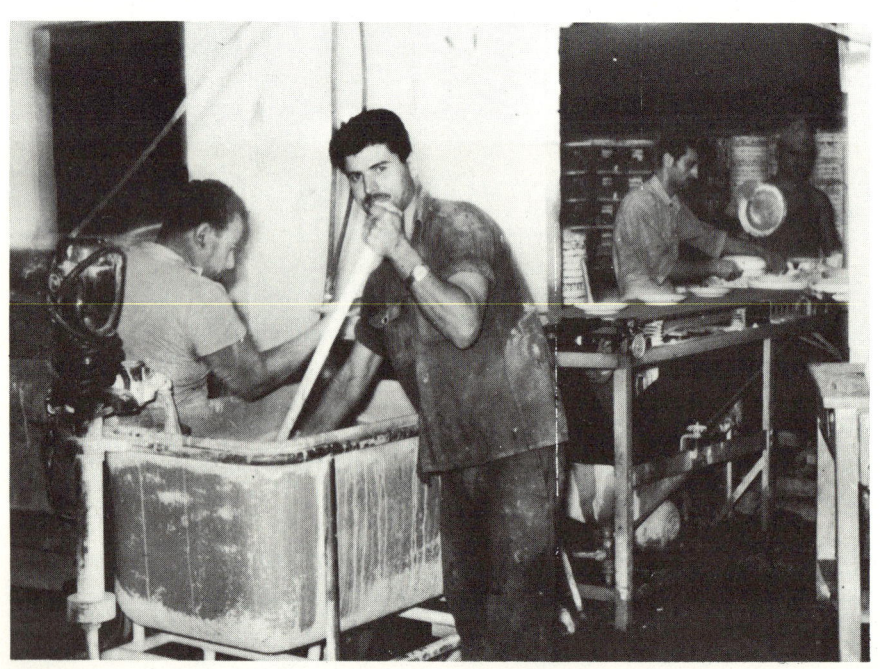

Jewish porcelain factory workers.

and their tendencies to become managers. He feels threatened by Sephardi-Oriental pressures on the Labor Federation because of their support of the Nationalist party. He hopes it will be possible to integrate all the workers and to make material progress through common effort.

At the factory, Shlomo and his comrades change into work clothes and go to the cafeteria for hot breakfast or midmorning snack, depending on the hour when they begin work. They can also eat hot lunch here, so that the old custom of a heavy noon meal and a rest at home has become an activity mainly for local tradesmen and office workers. The older men say that staying in the factory all day is "Americanizing" them for the benefit of the management. The feel that the pace should slow down because of the hot climate, at least until air conditioning becomes more prevalent. The work day ends by four in the afternoon, when the men can take a hot shower at the factory, as is the practice in the kibbutz. Their labor contracts specify such improved conditions so that they might return home as "gentlemen." They look down on those workers who do not clean up or change after work, and they call them "filthy Arabs," regardles of their origins.

Shlomo's work week begins on Sunday, which in Hebrew is called *Yom Rishon*, The First Day (of the Week). He works for five and a half days, until the mid-afternoon of the Sixth Day (Friday), which is approaching the Sabbath Eve. The Religious parties have had Sabbath transportation curtailed. Thus there is a major rush by workers and other travelers to arrive at their destinations before sundown when an atmosphere of Sabbath tranquility descends on the country. The two-day weekend has been rejected by officials and it has not been pushed by the Labor Federation although it has considerable influence on the government. They say the country's economic development will not support so much time off.

There are five Jewish religious holy day times, including extensive vacation periods during Passover in the spring and Succoth (Tabernacles) in the fall, also national holidays such as Israeli Independence Day, and half-holidays commemorating other traditional festivals and secular or political events such as May Day. Workers are frequently absent for the month-long military service and days within the month, sick leave, and personal affairs, which are entangled in bureaucratic procedures. While there is a national ideology concerned with productivity, in actuality the traditional practices and personal needs often interfere with work.

DOMESTIC DUTIES

Back home, Rivkah has cleared off the breakfast table rapidly. Her plastic dishes require less care than the new porcelain she purchased for holiday company. Most of her household goods are now locally produced and they can successfully compete in quality with the imports and, of course, in price. There is still status in purchasing gifts of foreign origin, but Israelis are pleased that their own products carry "snob" appeal overseas. Rivkah grabs a mop with a rag, called a *shmatah* and, using kerosene or a new detergent, she washes and cleans the tile floors of the apartment. She has remembered to remove the carpets and hopes she can beat them on the balcony before the neighbor puts out her wash below.

She would like to avoid the constant friction that takes place in apartment houses where some neighbors are inconsiderate. Good neighbors are an asset, especially if you need them to mind a small child who is not yet in nursery school.

Uri is a concern of Rivkah's and she must prepare him for the neighbor and his playmates before she can attend to her marketing. The child was born at the time of the Six-Day War at the Kupat Holim (Sick Fund) hospital in Naharya. At the time of his circumcision, which took place at home on the eighth day, a friend acted as godparent, and the child was named after a very pious great-uncle. The old man had migrated to Jerusalem to be close to the Western Wall of the Second Temple site, and he was buried on the Mount of Olives. The Jordanians had desecrated this Jewish cemetery until the liberation of Jerusalem by the Israeli Defense Forces during the 1967 War. The family keeps the black-bordered announcement of the old uncle's death which happened while they were still in Europe. The birth of Uri is for them a reminder of the reunification of Jerusalem after 2000 years, which is considered a miracle second only to the Independence of the State of Israel. Rivkah hopes Uri will become eligible for a day care center sponsored by the Labor Federation's Working Mothers' Organization or the WIZO, the Women's International Zionist Organization. She would not choose institutionalized care like that of the kibbutz, but she desires to supplement the family's income by working part-time in a textile plant. She also wishes to see to her motherly duty of being home when the children return from school; hence her dilemma.

Before midmorning, Rivkah is off to the Old City market where she can find bargains in food and where she might meet some of her friends and discuss family happenings. Rivkah notices that more Jews now operate shops in the Old City and that they have stocked them with Israeli manufactured products and have modernized their display counters. Prices are subject to government controls, so Rivkah patronizes shops not on the basis of prices but where she receives special attention and where the goods meet her standards for quality. She carries her groceries and produce in a basket or else in large plastic "string" bags. She may save some of the shopping for later when the children or Shlomo can help her carry the heavier items. In the market Rivkah mingles with country Arabs and townsmen who have come from many nations. She is able to make limited contact with them, but she reserves her more extensive conversations for her friends who are usually from the same background as she and Shlomo.

Rivkah prefers to purchase food that is fresh. She does not hesitate to tell the seller if his products appear to be stale or unwholesome. She checks the eyes of fish to see if they glisten and she looks for signs of blood or waste in the gizzard of chickens that are now cleaned and placed for sale. Rivkah can recall the time when she kept fish alive at home in pans or in the bathtub before refrigeration came. She did her own plucking of chickens after buying them directly from the slaughterer. Arab and Jewish farmers now sell their livestock through a wholesaler, but in Acre there is still a shepherd who grazes a flock near the Turkish walls. Refugees and immigrants kept cattle, sheep, goats, and poultry in the caravan-stops of the Old City. Today the Municipality makes certain that hygienic standards are observed in the shops and that the streets around are cleaned.

There are now regulations extending even to the dumping of waste into the harbor where it creates a nuisance and pollutes the beach below.

Although Rivkah was brought up to cook according to central European tastes, she finds that Oriental preparations are often better suited to Israel's climate and workers' budgets. Meat is especially expensive and it is made into stews, called goulash, or *cholent*, which is a casserole dish of meat and beans baked in the oven over the Sabbath. Rivkah's family now enjoys skewered meat that the Arabs call *shashliq* for beef, and *shish kebab* for lamb. They also like salads such as *humus*, which is made of chickpeas and sesame paste and Oriental vegetables such as squashes and eggplants that are stuffed with meat and rice. The fresh fish caught in Acre's bay is delicate when fried. Rivkah purchases carp, raised in kibbutz fishponds nearby, for her Sabbath *gefulte* fish balls. She does not favor canned foods, and frozen foods are found mainly in large city supermarkets. Desserts may be purchased or, preferably, made at home. Rivkah purchases European-style cream-filled cakes for special treats at coffee or teatime. Oriental pastries are considered quite sweet and are sampled when a neighbor brings them or serves them at a reception. Housewives now have ovens and no longer rely on the top-of-the-stove *wunder pot* for baking cakes for the Sabbath and festivals. The proud hostess awaits the comments of her guests about her layer cakes and cookies topped with nuts and raisins.

During her shopping, Rivkah notes that the stores are now displaying fashionable ready-to-wear clothing made in Israel. Knitted goods, rain gear, and leather products are exported and they are considered to be of high quality. The hot summer climate and the winter rains determine the family's clothing supply. Suits, coats, and leather shoes are considered to be major investments and they are purchased after careful family planning. Informal and brief attire for the summer months is reasonable in price. Rivkah does some home sewing for herself, but clothing for other members of the family is purchased. Variety of clothing has increased but so have the costs since the simpler times when Labor movement people wore khakis. The country is now more conscious of grooming and style and participates in international trade.

During her marketing Rivkah would like to sit down to talk with friends she meets, but Acre's cafes are for men and women must socialize while standing on the street or within shops. The beauty parlor is the one place where women may sit and have leisurely interchange. Otherwise, they plan visits together with their husbands for the early evening or on the Sabbath. There are few telephones among ordinary people so that casual meetings become occasions for learning about family events and for arranging hospitality. Full meals are still taken among family members, though celebrations such as weddings, confirmations, and religious festivals usually include close friends who may also be neighbors. Formal invitations for a celebration might be sent through the postal service or else delivered by children. The hosts must increase their food purchases unless they have a catered affair. The guests must make decisions about selecting a suitable gift. The wife will choose tiny baby garments, books, or bric-a-brac for the living room during her morning market trip. She will await her husband's company during the late afternoon or evening promenade for larger and for more expensive items. The good housewife is prepared for company at any time, but there are specific periods when visitors are less likely to call, such as during the heat of the day when the family and its guests from out-of-town are most likely to take their rest. The day and the week are divided into time-zones for private and for public interaction.

YOUTH CULTURE

The family's son, Danny, has entered the secondary school, which means that he is committed to technical or professional studies and the family must be concerned with tuition. Danny passed his qualifying examination with a high score, especially in mathematics. He had some trouble with language studies, English, and with literature, but his scores in Jewish philosophical and historical studies warranted advancing him with a partial scholarship. Danny did almost as well on his examination as children of white-collar and professional families in Acre. But most of the Sephardi-Oriental and many Ashkenazi workers' children did poorly. Some plan to learn trades in vocational programs. Several children in the neighborhood are leaving school at age fourteen, which is the minimal age at which this is permitted. Some may seek jobs through the Labor Federation's youth services. All are advised to attend further training classes in the evening, but most would prefer to earn money for themselves and their families until their military service, when they can gain new skills. Danny's family encouraged him to consider secondary school and perhaps college or university education to help him to reach his career goals. The teachers also encouraged Danny and they pointed out that the country needs skilled technical and professional persons (though it is not considered proper to downgrade the contributions of the factory workers).

Danny's social interests have begun to focus on his schoolmates and teachers and away from neighborhood and organized youth clubs. He had already toured the country and worked on a kibbutz while in the youth movement. In the secondary school he plans to join the Gadna, which is a premilitary training corps. This would make him eligible for higher rank when he enters military service after graduation. He and his companions in Gadna are also exposed to discussions about national defense policy and tactics and they visit installations and meet youths and leaders from all over the country. Danny has even thought about possible advanced training overseas, in America. He prefers the welfare democracy of Israel to, what he imagines to be, the materialistic life of capitalist America. He considers non-Jews to be anti-Semitic and large cities to be unsafe. But he admires the technical achievements of the United States and acknowledges that these would be useful if applied in Israel.

Danny and his friends show great interest in the problems of Israel even though they are close to their families. They consider the local affairs of the city of Acre much lower in priority, because they may not be remaining there. Danny thinks all Jews should live in Israel and help in its development. He recognizes the importance of American and other Diaspora Jewish support for the Ingathering of the Exiles and Israel's defense needs, but he thinks those communities will ultimately assimilate if they are not destroyed by another Holocaust. He is determined that Israel's sabra generation together with its veteran leaders will prevent a repetition of the Nazi genocide of the Jews. He greatly admires the vision of Chaim Weizmann and David Ben-Gurion, who brought about the birth of Israel. Though he denigrates most political party leaders as bureaucrats, he supports the new generation of Dayan and Allon who developed in the Defense Forces that fought the War of Independence and succeeded in securing new frontiers during the Six-Day War. He is less concerned with the ideological disputes between the right and the left and between secularists and religious parties than with preparation for defense and cooperation for survival. Thus, his identity is with the national level of affairs and is future-oriented.

Danny feels that the Arabs cannot be trusted and that they respond only to a show of strength. He thinks the Arabs of Acre have a sense of kinship with Israel's enemies in the neighboring countries and therefore they must be controlled. He would prefer for all Arabs to be settled beyond Israel's borders, but he realizes this would be disapproved by world opinion. He values the large numbers of Middle Eastern Jews in Israel because they have experienced persecution under the Arabs and they will fight to keep Israel strong. He has made friends with Sephardi-Oriental youth in the neighborhood and in youth groups, but lasting contact is reserved for those who have the ambition and the ability to accompany him into secondary school and the Gadna. Nevertheless, Danny feels a basic unity exists among all Jews and this is reinforced by the hostility of Arab neighbors and the Gentile (non-Jewish) world beyond.

Danny subscribes to a sabra ideology that is pragmatic in its idealism. His sense of manliness is based upon physical fitness to maintain good health, to better his mind through study, and to show concern for weaker people. He is competitive with his peers but he knows how to cooperate for group ends; he has been influenced by the spirit of the kibbutz, but he prefers more private life. Danny will challenge and negotiate on many issues, but he will also fight to the finish for what he considers to be essential decency. While he values all life, he would not hesitate to take one or to give up his own for a just cause. He does not care for government bureaucracy, but he recognizes that there must be order and that little is accomplished through anarchy. He respects the achievements of the older generation but he is impatient for his own generation to prove its merits. He is confident that Israel will succeed as a Jewish Homeland and as a leading force for world social justice. He awaits the time when Israel will be free from dependence on foreign gifts and the dictates of great powers. But he knows that a small people and a small nation require alliances just as the local government parties must form coalitions.

Miriam, the younger sister, attends grammar school in the neighborhood. She prefers her school to those in immigrant quarters because the pupils are more interested in their studies and aspire to go on to secondary school. Miriam meets immigrant neighborhood children at the youth club and some are in the Municipal Orchestra where she plays the flute. She finds the variety of Jewish children to be important for the development of the country and the city. But she agrees with her parents that she cannot spend time with everybody, so she plays with girls who are more serious about what they want to do in life. She respects her parents for their guidance and she also admires her sabra teachers and older girls who have had experience outside the city confines.

Miriam dreams of the day when she will do service in the Israel Defense Forces. She might become a teacher in a remote Oriental Jewish immigrant village. Or perhaps she will train as a nurse in a large hospital near Tel Aviv or Jerusalem. She would serve her people by helping them with their education and their health. This would be her fulfillment until she marries and has a family of her own. She prefers mixed company with sabras regardless of whether they are Ashkenazi or Sephardi. She would be willing to tend Arabs in a hospital setting, but she would neither date nor marry an Arab. She also wonders whether she would marry a religiously observant Jewish boy and whether such a marriage would restrict her mingling with a wide variety of people. Miriam believes that Jewish tradition can be carried out by living in Israel, but that rituals are less important than this. She would not marry and go to live in a foreign country like America though she might like to visit there sometime.

Miriam has many activities after school, which is dismissed in the early afternoon. After a snack, she completes her homework. Then she meets her girlfriends for a walk. She goes to the orchestra rehearsal in preparation for an early evening dedication ceremony for a new apartment building. Miriam does not question the fact that her orchestra is composed entirely of Jews. She notes that the Arabs have their own drum and bugle corps attached to their Scout troop. When she travels with her orchestra to distant cities to participate in a parade, she feels the group and its director are among the best in the land. But she resents it when the children in the other cities jeer the Acre contingent and say that it comes from "a city of Arabs and where the museum is in a crazy-house." She has no interest in Rotary club booklets on Acre's historical personages. Rather, she wishes the Municipality would clean up the city and make it as pretty as Naharya. She is resigned to growing up in Acre because her friends and her family live there. But she waits for the time when she can live amidst modern surroundings as a Jewish woman in the Jewish state. Such are the norms of youth culture, which imply loyalty to family and to one's people, but with freedom to select one's vocation and where one will settle down.

LEISURE TIME AND HOSPITALITY

As the workday draws to a close, the families gather at home to change clothing and to take tea and a snack before setting out for the customary early evening walk down the main street of the New City toward the Mediterranean Sea. Along the way, they window shop and plan for purchases that require budgeting. They exchange greetings with acquaintances who are doing the same thing. Some older men gather at a crossroads corner where they argue politics. Youths are on an opposite corner near the cinema where they make decisions about whether to attend the early or the late evening performance. The films are mainly American or European with Hebrew, Arabic, and French subtitles or dubbed in

Hebrew. The films' violence or romanticism provides an interlude from small apartment life and the factory or military service on the borders. Television has begun to make inroads on movie attendance and it has even begun to keep families at home after work. But the people crave the evening breezes and the chance of meeting friends and sharing bits of gossip, for they are gregarious.

Numerous food vendors along the street extend the evening stroll into suppertime and they cater to the tastes of all age groups. People stop for *felafel*, which is an envelope of *pitta* filled with deep-fried balls of chickpea paste and smothered with peppers, onions, and sauerkraut. Boiled sweet corn is sold in the summertime and the husks are strewn in the gutters. The people drink *gazoz* (*eau gaseuse*), which is carbonated water mixed with fruit syrup. They enjoy ice creams of assorted flavors and sherberts, which originated among the Arabs of the Middle East. On the streets and in the cinema the youths chew sunflower seeds to such an extent that many have worn a groove in their front teeth which causes lisping. Spitting seeds and nutshells is so widespread that adults have campaigned, though without much success, to have the authorities control the nuisance, at least on buses and in public places.

People who are visiting or who expect company return to their homes while the youth mill about for a few more hours. Adults spend the evenings on their balconies except in the middle of winter. They entertain company informally, serving snacks and wine or brandy, exchanging gossip, or playing cards. This lasts for only a few hours, because the workers retire well before midnight in anticipation of early morning rising. The last radio news and the shutdown of the Kol Yisrael broadcasting schedule takes place at 11 o'clock with the playing of *Hatiqvah* (Hope), the Zionist and Israeli anthem.

During the evening there also exists a more formal life in Acre, which is sponsored by the Municipality, the Labor Federation, political parties, and voluntary associations. The weekly newsletter advertises events that take place at the Municipal Culture Center, such as seminars in Jewish history and language study. Political parties announce the visit of national dignitaries. There are vocational courses and artistic programs for all groups in the city. For most activities only a core of the faithful attend, but for some famous speaker or performer the cinema hall or an auditorium or a cafe will fill to overflowing. Sabbath night is more popular than weekdays for such formal activities, and men are more likely to participate than their wives. The women are less likely to understand Hebrew programs and they prefer concert-stage to political speeches or seminars. The men may leave their wives visiting with women friends and return after the meeting to escort them home. The streets are considered to be safe, and they are quiet by 10 o'clock on weekday evenings. Young soldiers on leave and kibbutznicks board trucks to return to their quarters. Most workers head for bed and leave the cafes to small groups of youths who, on the morrow, will have to reckon with the daily work schedule, that is, if they are employed.

The week's routine for the sober working-class culture is punctuated by special family and neighborhood events that take place particularly during the summer vacation period. During the last fieldwork period, a North African postal carrier held a *bar mitzvah* reception in the *bustan*, or garden, of his Arab-style house at the edge of the New City. He had invited hundreds of his patrons and neighbors by word of mouth. His colleagues assisted in serving the long tables which groaned with platters of Oriental pancakes, vegetables, salads, beverages, and cakes. A small Moroccan band played through amplifiers and filled the air with music from Israel, the Mediterranean, and the Middle East. The Oriental men among the guests rose to dance and the westerners clapped to the rhythms with delight. Jews and Arabs toasted each other with *l'chaim*, "To Life," in honor of the young man who had read from the Torah in his communal synagogue that morning. Three generations of kinsmen had gathered from distant parts of the country. They spent several days catching up on family affairs and helping to prepare the foods for the evening reception. On the Sabbath there would be additional blessings and festivities at the synagogue and at home for a new son of Israel who had come of age.

More affluent and status-seeking families hold wedding receptions at cafes during weekday evenings in the summertime. Their circumstances and their pride influence the surroundings they select and the extent of the guest list. Many go into debt and the situation has become highly competitive and a cause for criticism by officials in government and their supporters. The Muslims hold a celebration for the men at the signing of the wedding contract. The reception for the bride is conducted in a cinema hall on Friday night. There is professional musical entertainment and the bride, the groom, and the bridesmaids are on stage as performers sing romantic ditties. The entire neighborhood feels involved in such celebrations and guests from different ethnic groups are given special welcome.

The most fulfilling domestic life and feelings of hospitality and community are ushered in with the Jewish Sabbath at sundown on Friday and extend until sunset of the seventh day of the week. Since Acre and Israel have a Jewish majority, the sacred days of rest for the Muslims and Christians continue, but with less impact on life in general than the holy days of the Jews. On Friday afternoon the family members and guests from out of town arrive home to bathe and to change into fresh clothing. Some men still go to public baths for steaming and for socializing, but these are falling into disuse in both Jewish and Arab quarters as indoor facilities become adequate. Meanwhile, the mother has been preparing for the Sabbath since Thursday's marketing and Friday's cooking and baking. Daughters help somewhat with housecleaning and with arranging for guests, but the main burden is on the hostess, which is expected and enjoyed.

The Sabbath has its basis in Jewish religion, but its celebration in the home by the nonreligious is universal, as if to affirm a common heritage among all the Jewish people. Religious men and children go to the synagogue together for prayers at sundown. At home, before sundown, the mother places candles in a pair of traditional silver or modern metallic candle holders, and she says a blessing for the kindling of the Sabbath lights. When the men and children assemble at the table, the host recites the *kiddush*, which is a blessing over wine for the day of rest. He then says a prayer over the *challah*, a braided egg-bread, and distributes pieces to all the company. An elaborate multicourse meal follows, with courses including soup, fish, vegetable dishes, and carbonated beverages according to ethnic custom. Traditional families sing religious melodies during the meal and conversation is kept as jocular as possible. The Sabbath meal ends with fruits and cake and hot beverages followed by a final grace, which is sung by traditional families.

Both secular and religious sectors of the community value the Sabbath tranquility and they put pressure on persons who make undue noise or who try to carry out commercial activities. There is more latitude in tourist areas and in Arab neighborhoods, but the general emphasis is on a change from daily routines. After the Sabbath evening meal, the young people depart for a stroll about the city. They meet with friends and perhaps join a group engaged in folk-singing or dancing at a club. There are restrictions on cinema performances and bus transportation, but nonreligious couples may drive their cars or take taxis to tourist cafes in Naharya or Haifa for musical entertainment and drinking. In the morning, while religious families attend synagogue, the nonreligious relax with weekend newspaper supplements and listen to classical music on the radio. Families arrange for picnics and trips to the beach if private or group transportation can be scheduled. Secular Labor and political organizations take immigrants and youths on historical tours of the region. Buses come to Acre's Old City and to the National museum in the old prison, and Arab *felafel* stands do a brisk business.

Crowds of people are strolling on the main thoroughfares as the Sabbath closes at sundown. Commercial activity and social intermingling reach new levels as acquaintances exchange greetings of *Shavuah Tov*, or "May you have a good week." Young people returning to military stations and other houseguests are escorted to the crowded bus stations or taxi stands. The cinema and the vendors nearby enjoy a crush of eager customers. This is the time when families are most likely to dine out at a cafe that serves Oriental skewered meats. More organizationally inclined adults may attend lectures sponsored by the Municipality or political groups. Others invite friends to come home with them for a final evening's drinking, conversation, and card games before thoughts must turn once more to the work week ahead. The people savor their Sabbath and festivals for they permit them respite from the intense domestic and industrial life that characterizes the development community and its national society.

7 / Ceremonial rounds

Public events, celebrations, and festivities range from traditional communal forms to secular and national expressions of identification. During the course of a year, Acre residents and visitors alike are impressed with the variety of public ceremonies that take place and which confer awareness on the immigrants both of the development city and of the national sponsors. These events occur during specific seasons of the year, tying religious practices to nature or commemorating major historical incidents. Many ceremonies relate the people to their local situation, while other ceremonies tie them to ethnic, religious, or national collectivities beyond the locality or even the State of Israel.

Minority and majority religious practices have their nationalistic ramifications. Secular approaches to intergroup relations and urban development are made through political celebrations. Local participation in welfare drives unifies the people of Acre and takes them from communal orientations to the larger issue of the place of the city in the national society.

The Municipality has recorded many of the ceremonies in its annual reports to document the progress of intergroup relations and urban development. It is possible to catalogue public meetings and to discover their sponsors and the times and places of celebration through the local bulletin, which is distributed with the weekend newspapers in the city. Many of the following ceremonies were observed during fieldwork.

MINORITY RELIGIOUS COMMUNAL LINKS

Religious festivals function as expressions of the solidarity among kinship groups, ethnic communities, and national collectivities. From the perspectives of intergroup relations in Acre and in Israel, the facts that the Arabs are now a minority and that communications with neighboring Arab countries have been disrupted, influence the practice of traditional festivals and give them more heightened nationalistic meanings than they might otherwise have. It is Israel's government policy to channel public recognition of all religious festivals through the Ministry of Religious Affairs. The Prime Minister's Office is also involved in public relations, attending receptions, and sending greetings in the name of the state. In Acre, the

Municipality expresses felicitations on behalf of the Mayor and the Council for local religious celebrations. Minority officials or appropriate representatives drawn from political supporters actually attend such festivals.

It is in the tradition of the Middle East to respect the diversity of religious activity as long as it is felt to be combined with a loyalty to the secular state. Thus, the Arab religious leaders invariably respond to greetings from public officials with expressions of civic loyalty. In view of the clash between Jewish and Arab nationalism, these manifestations of citizenship, civil rights, and civic loyalty are in essence subtle strategies by the minority as well as the majority and they have political overtones. Minority Arab religious celebrations thus reinforce their own communal solidarity. They also strengthen ties with coreligionists abroad and provide a measure of local intergroup relations. The circumstances of history and politics associated with Arab-Jewish nationalist struggle in the Middle East and the influence of the great powers are inevitably linked with these local religious events.

MUSLIM FESTIVALS

Muslim religious practices are derived from the Five Pillars of Islam, which are prescribed in the Koran and elaborated in Commentaries. There is little to restrict Acre's Muslims from subscribing to Faith, Prayer, Charity, and Fasting during the month of Ramadan, but it has been impossible for them to complete the Pilgrimage to Mecca because the Saudis refuse to admit Arabs from Israel, as they consider them to be collaborators. Alternative sacred sites are now accessible for Muslims in Jerusalem at the Mosques of al-Aksa and Omar, but these do not satisfy the commandment for Pilgrimage. Also, Jewish control of Jerusalem's ancient quarter is considered anathema to all Arabs, as well as Muslim and most Christian world leadership. Religious expression in the political context of Muslim and Arab life in Acre, Israel thus has important intergroup dimensions. Religious piety has diminished considerably among modern Arabs, but religious festivals have taken on the form of nationalistic affirmation and, above all, family expressions and recreational pursuit.

The religious calendar of the Muslims is unlike that of Christians and Jews in that it does not follow the agricultural seasons exactly. It has a lunar base but, since it lacks leap years, it is possible for festivals to move backwards through the solar cycle. The festivals thus occur at times widely different from the major Christian and Jewish festivals, which are more coordinated through the use of "leap" months for the Jewish lunar religious calendar. The Muslim religious festivals, being separated from those of the Christians and Jews, are even more divorced from the secular calendar, which dominates the world of work and the record of contemporary events. Nevertheless, religious community feelings of Acre's Muslims are reinforced through radio and television programs beamed from neighboring countries and Arab minority broadcasts on Kol Yisrael. Local people can identify with the celebrations taking place in Mecca and Cairo, Damascus and Jerusalem, and with their nationalistic implications.

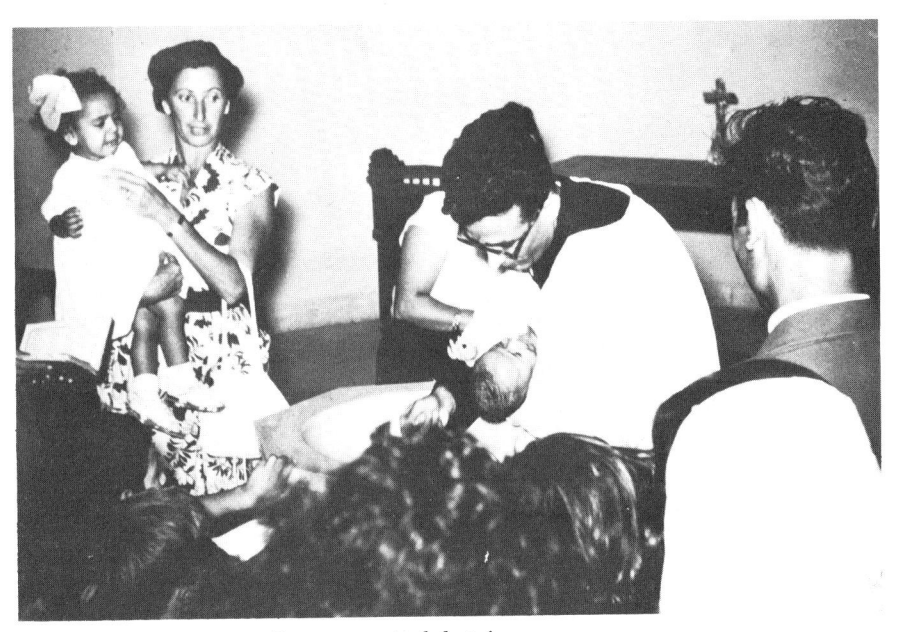

Protestant Arab baptism ceremony.

Muslim Arab celebrations in Acre are conducted through the Muslim Committee, which has its center at the Jazzar Mosque. The occasions are perhaps more political and social than sacred, but there are enlarged prayer services. Religious and political leaders represent the community in exhorting the government to restore property and other rights to Arab refugees and to provide more housing, employment, education, and other services for the minority residents in the city. These invocations are relatively mild compared with calls for *Jihad*, or Holy War, which come from Arab capitals abroad, but the Jews sense a relationship between local and international Arab aspirations against Israel. In actuality, the local Arab demands have been channeled through the democratic political process in Acre and in Israel and they assume strategies based on negotiation and bargaining rather than outright confrontation, but the Jews do not trust these either.

One of the major Muslim festivals is the Month of the Fasting, which is called Ramadan. Believers are expected to abstain from food during the daytime hours, but at night they dine and usually participate in other festivities. Manual workers find the obligation to fast during Ramadan especially difficult when it occurs during a season of hot weather, and it is said that tempers at this time are unusually high. The younger generation is less likely to observe the fast, but all members of the community rejoice at the 'Id al-Fitr, which marks the conclusion of the month. Families gather for relaxing meals and a display of affection and loyalty. There is an attempt to compensate for political and social disabilities by warm interpersonal relationships and pleasant local recreational pursuits.

The second major Muslim festival is the 'Id al-Adha, which is the Feast of the Sacrifice. This commemorates the culmination of the Hajj, the Pilgrimage to

Mecca, which is an obligation for faithful Muslims. In Arabia, the center of activity is the *ka'ba*, a Black Stone with a very ancient sacred mystique. There is also some recognition of the Semitic Patriarch, Abraham, whose son, Ishmael is the ancestor of the Arabs while his other son, Isaac, is the ancestor of the Jews. Since the 1948 Arab-Israeli War, the local celebrations of the festival focus on family and recreational pursuits. Only a few local persons seem publicly concerned about their inability to make the Pilgrimage to the sacred cities of Mecca and Medina, which are in Saudi Arabia.

Acre has not been a particularly religious center for Muslim Arabs. The Mosque of Jazzar and his tomb serve primarily as tourist attractions, rather than as places for religious pilgrimage. There is a shrine in the Shadliya Mosque that is sacred to a sect that originated in Tunisia. Cemeteries and occasional mausoleums and vaults have lost some personal meaning since the 1948 War and the flight of the original population. For their festivals, the local Muslim Arabs prefer to picnic by the sea or on the walls, or else to stroll through the public gardens and window shop along the main street of the New City. Outside the walls, there is a carnival atmosphere. Large swings are set up for children and they may take rides in donkey carts. Games of chance are promoted for older youths and men. The festivals permit the Muslim Arabs of Acre to set aside their work routines, but they are also reminded of their limited status since the Arab-Israeli wars.

CHRISTIAN FESTIVALS

Christian Arabs hold Christmas and Easter as their major festivals. These are celebrated locally as communal and family events in the context of their minority position. The celebrations are further fragmented because the Catholics follow the Gregorian calendar of western countries, while the Orthodox adhere to the Julian calendar of the old Eastern Roman Empire. This makes their festivals take place approximately one week later than their neighbors' celebrations. At these times, the television and radio remind local Christians that they are linked with world centers, such as the Vatican. For local Arabs, it is not too difficult to journey to Nazareth, where Christ lived. Major religious and social events draw pilgrims and other tourists here with the active approval of the government.

Since the 1967 war, it has become possible for Christian Arabs from Israel to circulate freely about Jerusalem's shrines and to visit in neighboring Bethlehem. The journey from Acre requires making overnight accommodations, which can be expensive, but it permits the reunification of dispersed kinsmen, since Christian Arabs come here from outside the country. Again, the government encourages this. When Jordan occupied Jerusalem's Old City and Bethlehem, between the 1948 and 1967 wars, it was frustrating for Israel's Christian Arabs to gain permits to visit these holy places. They made their pilgrimages in loyalty to their families but bore deep resentment of the political bureaucracy that impeded them.

Despite their double-minority status, both among Arabs and within the Jewish state, the Christians sense that they have leverage, as in the past, because of the support they receive from western countries. The Jews are mindful of the political implications of international Christian relations, and they are most circumspect in their dealings with local clergy and the hierarchy. Such prudence is sometimes difficult because the bishops both within the country and outside do not hesitate to criticize Israel's treatment of the Arabs and to call for the internationalization of Jerusalem. Local Arabs receive some financial support from overseas, but most important to them is the possibility of using religious channels for study and permanent residence as they become dissatisfied with local opportunities.

The heritage of Jewish-Christian relations in Europe contributes to guarded, if not hostile, intergroup feelings. Easter derives from the Passover seder in the Last Supper, and there are common symbols in the lamb, the unleavened bread, or wafer, and wine. But the Christians identify these symbols with the passion and death of their Saviour, Jesus, while the Jews literally link the symbols with the Exodus from Egypt many centuries ago. During Holy Week in Europe, especially in the Russian-dominated sectors, Jews were accused of using the blood of Christian children in the making of the unleavened bread. The Czars utilized such myths to create an atmosphere that led to pogroms, where Jewish communities were massacred by local peasants led by priests. Such memories prevent the Jews from recognizing the beauty of the Christians' spring festival. Jews in Israel and Acre also separate themselves from Christmas and the New Year even though Nazareth is not far away. Tourism is encouraged, of course, and appropriate seasonal greetings are exchanged, but the Jews celebrate Hanukkah as a freedom festival

Greek Orthodox wedding.

at this time and gigantic *menorahs* (candelabras) in all settlements simulate the lights that push back the darkness of the winter and revitalize historical memories.

Special religious anniversaries mark Christian life in Acre and bring it recognition from other Arab community groups and from coreligionists who live elsewhere in the district. Saint George's Day, for example, is celebrated by Acre's Greek Orthodox community in their famous church, which dates back to the city's revival in the seventeenth century, after centuries of neglect following the collapse of the Crusader Kingdom. The church and its community continue in the traditions of the Eastern Orthodox Church and the heritage of Byzantium and Constantinople, and local decorations include eastern-style depictions of Saint George slaying the dragon. However, the significance of Saint George in Christian theology and the historical role of the Eastern Roman Empire and its successors are lost on the Arabs gathered at the celebration. For them, the saint's day gives excitement to lives that are otherwise mundane and it also reinforces their sense of community identity. In the morning, they assemble in their church with their many guests who come from all Arab sects, including Muslims. The mass is celebrated by the venerable white-bearded diminutive priest in black cassock and round hat. He has gained his reputation by representing the Arab minority in Acre in its dealings with military government in the past. He is supported by laymen who have been active both in the coalition government and in the Communist opposition. He is respected by the younger generation, who must decide between adjusting to the working-class society or leaving for a new life elsewhere.

In Saint George's Orthodox Church, on a springtime Saturday morning during the fieldwork period, huge white candles flanked the eastern-style painting of the Madonnna and Child. The flames were reflected in the silver and brass ornaments and icons that were suspended in the naves of the church. Women, dressed in gowns of pastel or cotton print, sat toward the center of the church. The men were clothed in suit coats and open-necked shirts, while only a few guests wore traditional head covering. The men sat in or else stood by high-back arm chairs, which surrounded the center of the church. Christian clergy and Arab dignitaries from many groups in their dark garb occupied places of prominence. During the ceremony, Christian and Muslim scouts in khaki marched into the church. They bore their distinguishing religious emblems along with the international banner of the scouts. The national flag was not presented, nor were there any Jewish representatives in attendance. Perhaps Jews were unlikely to participate in a Christian religious ceremony, particularly on the Jewish Sabbath. Yet, this day of rest for the Jewish majority permitted many Arab workers to participate in their own communal activity, since their factories and shops were closed. The mass lasted for several hours and the assembly chanted the responses. There was no sermon nor other speechmaking. When the service was completed shortly after noontime, the people exchanged farewells and departed in clusters for further visiting at home and feasting. The celebration had brought family and neighbors together, which seemed sufficient for their wants.

JEWISH RELIGIOUS FESTIVALS REINFORCE ZIONISM

The origins of Jewish religious festivals lie in the agricultural life of the Jewish homeland and the theological interpretations given to historical or legendary events that occurred in ancient times. The unity of the Jewish people has always been stressed with emphasis placed on kinship. Jewish religion is very much this-worldly, but it has manifested messianic characteristics during periods of extreme oppression by powerful imperial conquerors. To a large degree, the religious and spiritual origins and drive of Zionism express the aspirations of a dispersed people, as stated in the anthem, Hatiqvah (Hope), which has been adopted by the political State of Israel. The establishment of the State has made the territorial aspects of the religious life more meaningful than its practice in the lands of the Diaspora. The reunification of Jerusalem in 1967 and the accessibility of the Western Wall of the Second Temple have permitted Jews to fulfill obligations of pilgrimage and thus affirm a sense of religious and national continuity.

The festivals have their communal aspects, but they have been given broader ethical interpretations. The "Chosen People" theme supports Zionism in characterizing the Jews as a nation among nations and an example for achieving world social justice. The celebration of Jewish religious festivals in Israel thus combines the linkage of the Jews to their Land with universal aspects. While the Religious parties appear to dominate the prescription of appropriate public recognition of the religious festivals, the other parties also join in their celebration in order to create a feeling of unity that is both national and worldwide. The schools explain the meaning of the festivals for the younger generation in more nationalistic and philosophical ways than is done at family celebrations, which are essentially ritualistic and recreational.

The holiest religious festivals are Rosh Hashanah, the New Year, and Yom Kippur, the Day of Atonement, which occur at the end of summer and before the cooler days of fall. These holy days are somewhat divorced from agricultural life and are spiritual in emphasizing man's relations to God and to his fellow men. Religious Jews and immigrants have strong memories of these holy days, with their emphasis on individual sins against God's commandments, the notion of divine redemption, and the historical record of martyrdom of the Jewish people. In Acre, as in most other Israeli towns, makeshift synagogues abound in cinema halls and public buildings because everyone with any religious inclinations attends. The Bureau of Religious Affairs acknowledges the temporary nature of this expanded religious activity, but it does its duty in supplying Torah scrolls and offering guidance where necessary. The congregations fast on Yom Kippur and they recite memorial prayers for deceased members of their families and for Jews who have died for the Sanctification of God's Name. This part of the service is especially poignant for Jews who experienced the Nazi holocaust, and indeed for all Ashkenazim. The Sephardi-Oriental celebration of the holy days is highly communal and brings together the generations.

The role of these important holy days in the life of Israel's growing secular generation of sabras has yet to be determined. The Socialist kibbutzim have had special difficulty in assimilating the essentially religious meaning of these holy days. Yet they feel that they should recognize these essentially religious holy days as symbols of the unity of the Jewish people, their common heritage, and ethical teachings. The 1973 Yom Kippur War should fix such group response.

In contrast, the agricultural pilgrimage festivals, such as Passover, have brought together all sectors of the society. Living a Jewish life in Israel expands the significance of these festivals beyond their traditional religious base. The Passover comes in the spring and is celebrated in a family setting at home, as well as in the synagogue and community. On the first evening, there is a ritualistic meal, called a *seder* (order), whereby the father is expected to recount the story of the Jewish Exodus from Egypt for the next generations. The mother has prepared special foods, which have symbolic significance, and has arranged them so that during the service they can be explained. The service is recited from a Hagadah (Narrative) according to the melodies familiar to the different Jewish ethnic groups that have developed over time. All members at the gathering participate at various periods during the seder. They are drawn together as a household and as a community with a long heritage and with a linkage to Jewish communities around the world and especially in the Jewish Homeland, according to God's Promise to the Children of Abraham.

The Passover celebration emphasizes that the Jews had once been slaves who were brought into freedom through their belief in God and in their loyalty to His commandments as a People. The ritual foods of the seder emphasize the *matzoth* (unleavened bread), which showed the haste with which the Children of Israel had to depart from Egypt. Four cups of wine commemorate the departure and promises of salvation. A fifth cup is dedicated to the Prophet Elijah who foretells the coming of the Messiah. A lamb-shank recalls the instructions to the Israelites to smear the blood of the sacrificial lamb on the door posts of their houses so that the Angel of Death would "pass over" them in avenging the first born of the Egyptians during the Tenth Plague. Parsley and egg represent sustenance, while horse-radish is a bitter herb to recall the period of servitude. All these symbols are explained during the ritual, according to accounts in the Bible and with rabbinical commentaries down through the ages. Families are expected to add their own explanations and draw from their personal experiences, whose analogies are many. Secular gatherings, particularly in kibbutzim, make innovations, but keep to the basic freedom theme along with the symbolic seder plate.

The community aspects of the Passover season encourage intergroup relations among Jews in Israel and an involvement in the country's development through knowledge, particularly of its historical and agricultural aspects. On the second night of Passover, the religious and political organizations of Acre sponsor "second seders," which bring the different Jewish ethnic groups together and encourage them to mingle with veteran settlers, perhaps at neighboring kibbutzim. In Acre, on the seventh day of Passover, the religious leaders of the Ashkenazi and Sephardi-Oriental communities join in a March to the Sea, in the evening, to commemorate Israel's passage out of Egyptian bondage. The traditional celebration thus becomes part of contemporary life, with its messages of freedom and

Jewish youth at Lag b'Omer campfire.

redemption linked to Zionist effort. These achievements are seen by youths on their week-long tours at this time.

The reinforcement of the relationship between religious festivals and the development of the Jewish Homeland appeals to Jewish youth. There are other springtime festivals associated with the barley harvest and with the gathering of "first fruits" after the rains have ceased and the clear and hot weather of May and June produces a bounteous variety of melons, green vegetables, tomatoes, and other produce. The autumn festival of Succoth has already been described (in Chapter 4) as a harvest celebration involving Ashkenazim and Sephardi-Orientals. The holiday permits a weeklong vacation with further tours of the countryside and historical sites. The schools introduce the historical and ethical significance of the religious festivals in their programs, and the children are encouraged to produce essays, works of art, and dramatic skits.

The children's celebrations of "minor" festivals emphasize the themes of freedom and Jewish self-determination. Heroes and heroines and villains emerge from the recounting of legend and history while at parties in schools and at clubs the children dress in appropriate costumes. Hanukkah (Dedication) takes place in the winter time and is symbolized by gigantic candelabras (Menorahs), by games of chance, and pancakes, which may have nourished the heroic Maccabees who fought against the Hellenists who wanted the Jews to assimilate. In the Temple, an oil lamp was discovered, which lasted for eight days during the rededication period. The families and communities celebrate the festival by kindling the lights each evening, adding one candle or lamp on each successive night. Purim (Lots) occurs early in the spring and reminds the Jews of how tenuous their security was under the usually benevolent rulers of Persia in ancient times. Queen Esther and her uncle, Mordecai, are imitated by countless boys and girls, while all assembled make loud noises as the wicked Haman's name is mentioned in the Scroll of Esther, which is read at this time. Later in the spring, the Jewish revolts against the Romans under Bar Kochba and others are recalled in gatherings in groves planted by the Jewish National Fund. The boys fashion bows and arrows, and groups perform folk dances and light fires in many outdoor places. These festivals promote community fellowship and serve as a link between past, present, and future.

LABOR CELEBRATES MAY DAY

The predominant political force in Acre and in Israel is Labor, which celebrates its international holiday, the First of May, together with socialists throughout the world. The Marxist red flag regularly flies over the Labor Federation headquarters in Acre, but on the First of May it joins the blue and white Zionist-Israeli national flag over the Municipality as well. The flag lacks the hammer and sickle of the Communists, for it represents Israel's link with international socialism rather than with totalitarian communism. The pioneers of the country came from nineteenth century labor-oriented movements in Europe that emphasized democracy and from this originated the agricultural communes and the Labor Federation which have had such impact on local development. The Labor parties must absorb the masses of Sephardi-Oriental immigrants and they must make the Labor Federation meaningful to young European Jews and to Arabs alike. We have already noted how Labor officials incorporate religious festivals into their Zionist programs through hospitality and tours. On the First of May, they make an accounting to the immigrants and the new generation of their achievements in the past and their programs for the present and the future. To this end, the Labor Federation publishes and distributes an annual booklet with statistics and illustrations of the year's events.

The annual celebration of the First of May in Acre begins with a parade of officials and youths in the afternoon and climaxes with a cinema hall review of achievements and musical entertainment. The parade is made up of contingents representing the several political divisions within the General Labor Federation. These groups emphasize greater or lesser degrees of public ownership, secularism, and nationalism. There is now an increasing involvement of hitherto anti-Labor Nationalist parties, which appeal to the Middle Eastern Jewish immigrants. The Communists and the Socialist Religious Zionists do participate in the General Labor Federation, but they did not participate in the celebration that took place during the fieldwork period. They held their own observances at different times and places, which signified the fragility of Labor's coalition in its attempt at widespread appeal to sectarian groups.

Labor's divisions and its inability to communicate to extremists and to youth were apparent during the evening performance on May Day observed during fieldwork. The stage of the cinema hall was filled with local officials and guests. The leaders expounded at length on the active role of the Socialist and the Labor movements in the building of the Jewish Homeland and in the absorption of the

Jewish immigrants. The Arab spokesman cited the need for peaceful solutions to the Arab-Jewish problems of Acre and hence the Middle East. Some guests who represented splinter parties berated the dominant party, MAPAI, for dealing with West Germany. The response was an attack on left-wing groups for supporting Russia who was backing Israel's enemies. Like all groups in Israel, the leaders of Labor are pragmatic and recognize that their policies and programs depend on good relations with the democratic West. Russia is recognized for having rescued Jews from the Nazis and for its contributions to the birth of the State of Israel in 1948.

The young people in attendance waited through the ideological expositions until the musical performances. These were highlighted by satirical skits that recalled the all-too familiar bureaucratic entanglements that are alleged to characterize the Labor movement. Youth's identification with the victims of bureaucracy clearly indicated their perceptions of the Labor Federation as "establishment" with limited mobility for young aspirants to office. The growth of left-wing and right-wing factions within the General Labor Federation is a reaction by ethnic minorities toward its middle-aged European Jewish domination.

Acre's Communists tried to present their own version of May Day in a separate celebration near the sea. Their Jewish and Arab leaders arranged a sound truck that was accompanied by youths who were mostly Arab. The truck was stationed near Sephardi homes on the Sabbath at a time in the afternoon when pajama-clad workers were trying to catch a nap. Besides interrupting the Sabbath peace, the presence of Arabs antagonized the Sephardi youths of the neighborhood so that the police had to intervene to prevent bloodshed. The Communists were accused of favoring Russian support for Egypt. In successive years, Jews have withdrawn from the party, especially since 1967, so that it has become identified with the Arab nationalist cause. The majority of Acre's Arabs still feel they can achieve more by working within the major Labor coalition. The threat of Arabs supporting the Communists gives them leverage with the Labor leadership.

NATIONAL IDENTITY PROBLEMS ON ISRAELI INDEPENDENCE DAY

The celebration of Israeli Independence Day is associated with the 1948 Arab-Israeli War. This limits the participation of Arab citizens and it poses a challenge to the government to give the new Jewish immigrants a sense of involvement. The holiday takes place early in May and is scheduled on the anniversary date according to the Hebrew calendar. It has incorporated military themes, which has drawn international criticism, particularly for parades scheduled in the holy city of Jerusalem. The holiday celebration includes ceremonies honoring the war dead, official reports of achievements in development during the past year, festivities for youth, and receptions for sectarian and minority groups and foreign guests. In Acre, the diminishing number of veteran settlers holds a celebration in a private home removed from the crowds of immigrants and youths.

The memorial service takes place on the morning preceding Independence Day. In Acre there is a parade of officials and school children from the Municipality to a war memorial stone tablet in the public garden. Contingents in the parade bear wreathes in honor of those members of the Haganah (Israeli Defense Forces) who fell in the liberation of the Galilee. Among the marchers are Arabs from the Municipality and the Labor Federation and scouts from the government-supervised orphanage. A wailing siren announces the traditional Jewish Memorial prayer service. The participants cover their heads and a cantor chants the ritual. Most Jewish citizens who attend this ceremony have not had any relatives in this war. Their most vivid memories concern the victory of 1967, which is celebrated a month later. Events of 1973 will be memorialized now on Yom Kippur.

Arab involvement in the Israeli Independence Day celebration is discrete. At the government school, officials bring greetings to the children and there are festive programs and refreshments. The boys perform gymnastics and the girls sing Arabic songs which all enjoy. Terra Sancta school is not involved in Israeli Independence Day ceremonies, although the Franciscan clergy attend the reception for community leaders, which is held on the afternoon of the holiday at the seaside tourist cafe. Arab youths are attracted to the fireworks near the seashore and to the street dancing on Independence Day evening as spectators. They keep their thoughts about this day within the confines of their homes or else in the cafes. They are exposed to television and radio broadcasts from Arab countries whose leaders use this occasion to inveigh against the existence of the State of Israel.

The local celebration of Israeli Independence Day appeals mainly to the immigrant families. Veteran settlers and sabras try to attend the major parades in Israel's metropolitan centers. They bring back stories about the new military displays, which permit Israel to maintain its defensive superiority over its Arab enemies. Now the television screen brings these parades into the homes of Jews and Arabs. Local Jews are able to identify with their nation's development, but the Arabs are confused about their civic role.

THE INTEGRATING ASPECTS OF ELECTIONS

The political campaigns that occur approximately every four years emphasize the role of Acre in Israel's development policies for Jewish immigrant absorption and Arab minority relations. National party leaders tour the Galilee during the daytime and come to Acre on the summer and early fall evenings where they meet the people out in open fields or else in the auditoriums of institutions or the cinemas. There is a constant coming and going at the open-air meetings, which take on a form of recreational activity for young and for old. They come to see such "stars" as David Ben-Gurion, Moshe Dayan, Golda Meir, the Nationalist Beigin, and others whom they have heard so much about. The leaders promise to continue government support for local development needs. They justify often controversial foreign policy decisions on the grounds of national security considerations. They exhort the public to reduce imports and luxury living at home so as to reverse the imbalance in foreign exchange and to enable the country to free itself from overseas aid. They urge the workers to utilize the channels of the Labor Federation to negotiate their demands rather than to resort to frequent strikes. The approach is institutional, even when local issues are discussed, such as sanitation, tourism, employment, education, religious facilities, housing, commercial centers, services to the elderly and to youth, and measures to halt the exodus of veteran settlers.

All residents of the city and the country engage in political activities. There are many different political parties representing ideological and pragmatic approaches to national development and they provide varying benefits to their diverse constituencies. The public seeks personal relations with the leadership and it accepts the bureaucracy with reluctance. Local political activity mirrors that of the nation. It has a large Arab minority and it continues to receive Jewish immigrants from European and Middle Eastern countries. The coalition of Labor and Religious parties cannot be certain of its power among these groups for there is a strong pull towards extremist political affiliation with Communist and Nationalist opposition parties. Local youth must also be wooed, for the better educated no longer identify with traditional working-class issues and the alienated and unskilled attack the power and privileges of those who have benefited the most from the Labor movement. Campaigning is extremely competitive and it emphasizes personalities as well as issues that concern varying groups in different ways. National and local elections occur approximately every four years in the fall, and these are preceeded by elections to the General Labor Federation, which give a clue to the feeling of the electorate toward the groups in power.

The election campaign of 1965 was observed during the fieldwork. Newspaper accounts of previous elections and the recent elections of 1969 and 1973 provide comparable materials. These confirm the general observation that in the long run the older settlers and the immigrants and the minorities all prefer a coalition of

Freedom party campaign meeting.

Labor and Religious parties. They approve a moderately strong pro-western international orientation, a social democratic domestic policy, and a continuing search for ways to negotiate with Arab neighbors while maintaining a strong defense force. The campaigns are accompanied by colorful posters, which are placed on innumerable billboards and buildings and which emphasize the Hebrew or Arabic letters of the alphabet that serve as the party symbols. Local candidates address gatherings in public meeting places, on street corners, and in homes. They are surrounded by aides who are young aspirants for jobs and who have useful family and neighborhood connections. All these local political people gain in status when they become a welcoming committee for famous leaders of the national parties who head the party lists and who visit Acre to explain their goals and the place of the city in the development plans of the country.

The actual elections which were observed took place in November 1965 under the supervision of the Ministry of the Interior. Seats in the Municipal Council (and the National Assembly) were distributed according to a system of proportional representation. The "key" to the local Council coalition was delayed until the National Assembly formed its own coalition which gave the inaugural ceremonies in Acre's Municipal Culture House a somewhat tentative atmosphere. The contest had been fought with the usual rancor and personalities had been subject to abuse. Hence the local officials feared, justifiably, it turned out, that local "friends" might not be able to serve together in a coalition while "enemies" would be forced to work together. Compromises would have to be worked out among Labor Federation leaders and interests among Sephardi and Arab aspirants.

The inauguration provided a portrait of Acre's leadership assembled to work out arrangements for self-government in an atmosphere of pervasive factionalism. A table was arranged for the Councilmen at the center of the room by Municipality staff who scurried about to make certain all arrangements were proper. The clergy sat at the front on one side of the room and the Labor Federation officials sat on the opposite side. The local official from the Ministry of the Interior presided from a platform and he began by reading a letter from the outgoing Mayor, who had left for an official position in Tel Aviv. The message called for stronger efforts in Arab-Jewish and Sephardi-Ashkenazi relations and less political factionalism. A coalition of Labor and the Religious parties among the Councilors voted in the new Mayor. Deputy Mayors were selected from among the leaders of the coalition parties. In 1965, the Mayor was a lawyer who had served many years as Municipal clerk and was of Syrian-Jewish extraction. Deputy Mayors included a Muslim Arab and Ashkenazi and Sephardi Religious party leaders.

In his inaugural message the incoming Mayor emphasized the importance of civic unity above partisanship. He recommended an increase in neighborhood associations in order to encourage local participation on a basis other than ethnicity or class. The Arab Deputy Mayor, speaking in Arabic, called for peace and progress. The Arab Labor Federation leader used Hebrew to articulate demands for greater recognition of the Arabic language for public affairs and increased services for children, housing, institutions, and intergroup relations. The Religious party leader called for greater sensitivity and respect for the Sabbath and religious practices and he promised cooperation through the coalition.

Strong criticism of the coalition came from the left and the right. The Arab Communist leader spoke in Arabic and then in Hebrew. He indicted the Labor Arab coalition members for inaction on such problems as overcrowding in the Terra Sancta school, dangerous housing conditions, needs for the fishermen's port, and tax relief for low income families. He also argued for international peace and good will. The right-wing Nationalist party leader noted how his movement had grown as a challenge both to the Religious bloc and to the Marxist Laborites. He wondered how the new Mayor would be able to rise above his party obligations and serve all the city.

A partial response came during the 1967 wartime crisis, when the Nationalist party and extreme Labor Zionist, but not Communist, parties joined in a "wall-to-wall" coalition. However, *status quo* was resumed a year or so after the victory of the Israeli Defense Forces and the Mayor was subject to extreme forms of factionally-inspired criticism.

There was such malaise by the time of the 1969 elections that the national leadership of the Labor party was called upon to help search for appropriate local mayoral candidates. A highly regarded civil servant could not be accepted because he was identified with the MAPAM Marxist Labor group, though he performed valuable service as treasurer for the city administration. Some Arab participants in the coalition became uneasy with the lack of progress toward peace and the repercussions from increasing terrorist activities which included their youth. The coalition has incorporated veteran bureaucrats to its elective offices, but it must also make way for ambitious Middle Eastern Jews and the youth of Acre. (See Appendix B for a comparison of 1969 and 1973 elections.)

COMMUNITY WELFARE EXTENSION

Although economic and political affairs bring the diverse people of Acre together in common pursuits, a stronger measure of local self-image is to be found in the giving of welfare aid both within and outside the locality. It is traditional among the three religious faiths represented in Acre to consider charity, called *zaka* in Arabic and *tsadakah* in Hebrew, essential attributes of the religious life. The Israeli government has institutionalized welfare through its ministries and it has incorporated gifts from coreligionists and nations overseas for local purposes. Local religious groups and volunteer organizations affiliated with Labor and the other political parties channel welfare aid to families in need and especially the elderly. Services for the sick are provided by government agencies together with the sick funds of Labor and other insurance groups and philanthropic support from overseas.

During the fieldwork period there was concern for social services and recreational programs for the elderly. A Parents' Home was dedicated by the Jewish community. The Muslim and the Christian Arabs were also preparing similar day-care centers for the elderly, and these were encouraged by government and local agencies and public subscription for funds. As the Ashkenazi rabbi nailed a *mazuzah* to the doorpost of the Jewish clubhouse, he remarked that "One man can rear ten sons today but ten sons cannot help one old man." Old age brought loneliness because the generations could not really live together, even though they were often forced to share overcrowded apartments. The programs emphasized both traditional and modern recognition of obligations within major ethnic groupings.

The people of Acre are even more concerned with the welfare of children. The many local kindergartens and programs for recreation attest to this. The problem of Crippled Children is even more heartrending, though its incidence is far less than the daily need to provide nutrition and modern guidance services. Nevertheless, it is the annual drive for Israel's ILAN, the Crippled Children's Fund, that has captured the spirit of all groups in the city and brought them together to present a significant donation to the national organization. This effort is unique in that it is not a government activity nor is it particularly ideological or part of the absorption or development program. It seems to represent a maturation of the local population in extending itself beyond personal or local needs or even identifiable recipients. Leadership comes from the middle-class Rotary Club, and from its women's auxiliary, which are both quite modern in outlook. The collection of funds and the attendant publicity follow national guidelines. The local leaders organize a mammoth parade down the main street of the New City in order to demonstrate to outsiders that the city is willing to make a significant contribution to such a worthwhile effort and that this should be reported.

In Acre, the first parade for the Crippled Children's Fund took place on a Saturday night late in May 1965 and it brought all parts of the population together as participants and as spectators. On the reviewing stand sat the Mayor, the Chairman of the local chapter of Rotary International, and the Labor Federation Executive Secretary. The scouts and the political youth movements provided marchers, along with the Municipal Orchestra. Equipment came from the Red Shield of David ambulance corps and from police and Accident Prevention educational units. A sound truck was in operation near the reviewing stand with leading citizens and institutional officials prepared to announce the size of their donations. There was an atmosphere of friendly competition as it was proclaimed that the Municipality employees had donated 75 Israeli pounds (worth about 35 hours of work); Labor Federation staff gave 50 pounds as did the bank workers; the Muslim Committee donated 60 pounds; and many individuals gave ten pounds each. The announcements drew varied comments from the crowd but, on the whole, people felt that the city was taking its rightful place in the national society and thus it should receive recognition.

The public ceremonies that take place in a development city like Acre reveal the pull of tradition and sectarianism against more secular and cosmopolitan efforts at unity. The religious celebrations perpetuate the separation of Muslim, Christian, and Jewish groups, though Ashkenazim and Sephardi-Orientals are coming together. Labor, which could provide ties across religious lines, is the center for political coalition but it has not absorbed many youths or persons of lowest or highest social mobility. The political system invites all families to participate and it accords them proportional representation. Yet factionalism threatens the inherent stability that has characterized the government of the country and the city while local groups search for charismatic leadership. Israel's experiences in war are bringing generations of Jews together while, on the other hand, they accentuate the dilemma of Arab youth. A spirit of community cutting across ethnic and religious identifications is shown in the welfare drive for the Crippled Children's Fund. Other than this welfare drive, there is little expression of local unity that does not evoke separatist feelings in the participants.

8 / Achieving community identity

The identity of the city of Acre during the Israeli period emerges as a combination of expectations held by public policy makers, the residents, and visitors. Residential groups have varying perceptions of the city, according to their ethnic, class, and generational affiliations. Visitors to Acre are influenced by what they see or are shown and by reports, brochures, and articles from official and journalistic sources that emphasize the relics of the past and development problems in the present. National and local officials are concerned with the degree to which the city has fulfilled such major policy objectives as Jewish immigrant absorption, working out appropriate Jewish majority–Arab minority relations, socializing the new generation, and promoting an appearance to the outside world that links history and folklore to industrial development.

A symbolic interpretation of the community process in Acre is provided by the Municipal Emblem and actual situations observed during the fieldwork period. The Emblem consists of quadrants depicting the present and the future in terms of a factory and a housing complex. The past is represented by an ancient sailing vessel and the sea wall. The factory symbol can be seen as Acre Steel City, the major industrial enterprise in the vicinity. Wolfson Housing Estate is the largest apartment development for immigrants. The symbol of the sea wall brings to mind the role of the old Turkish citadel, which was used as a prison by the British and which has been converted into a national museum by Zionist groups with government support. The sailing vessel is a reminder of Acre's historical role as a port and future plans for developing the Old City for tourist purposes.

Acre's image derives mainly from the population's evaluation of services that are locally performed. This is not a "community" in the traditional sense of long-term commitment or affection on the part of residents. The activities associated with the Municipal Emblem reveal Acre as an old-new city on the shores of the Mediterranean in the vortex of nationalistic struggle in the Middle East. Groups concerned with the development of Acre assess these events according to personal and public standards. Some feel that they benefit while others are alienated. The city and its national society have a limited capability of meeting the needs and expectations of the population and making Acre attractive to visitors and investors.

ECONOMIC ADAPTATION THROUGH ACRE STEEL CITY

Following the establishment of the Jewish state, the government brought together overseas Jewish investors and Labor Federation interests to develop Acre Steel City. They planned an industrial enterprise that would process scrap metals to meet national defense needs, agricultural development, and construction in the cities. They also wished to provide employment for immigrants to facilitate their absorption. Professional analysts selected a site on underutilized land situated within easy rail distance of Haifa port and where a large labor force was available. An industrial zone was created before the walls of Acre. This enabled the government to promote a large Jewish immigration, as was official policy for districts with significant Arab populations (though Arabs were not employed in Acre Steel City for security reasons).

The Municipality of Acre was generally pleased to have Acre Steel City as a source of employment for the growing population and it was proud of the enterprise, as a sign of modernity and progress. The Labor Federation benefited with the growth of workers and their labor unions. The Labor parties felt comfortable that the management of Acre Steel City was controlled by the General Labor Federation and its subsidiaries. They felt that this followed the ideology of a Cooperative Commonwealth, i.e., basic Labor Zionist philosophy. Local tradesmen generally benefitted from the employee payroll that was generated by Acre Steel City, as did the families of workers and other service personnel. Visitors to the city were shown how it was possible to integrate a historical site with industrial development. It was emphasized to tourists that foreign and domestic planning and capital investment had cooperated to produce this essential enterprise in the national and the local interest.

Acre Steel City has also had its critics on the national and local level. Spokesmen from the Herut Freedom party attacked the original proposal in the National Assembly because it enhanced the power of Labor through their participation in capital investment and management. They questioned economic soundness of the process by which scrap metal would be converted into pipes because the materials and the fossil fuel used in the plant would have to be imported. Their predictions that costs would be exorbitant and noncompetitive were borne out during the first decade of operation. The managers requested government subsidy and began to curtail production. The Municipality and the Labor Federation pressured the government to prevent a shutdown. At the same time they demanded alternative industrial development to prevent massive unemployment, demonstrations, political defection, and a slowdown in further Jewish immigration. Fortunately, it was possible to attract investment capital from West German reparations payments, Israeli bonds, and Labor and private sources and to establish a variety of small and medium-size plants for chemical and food processing, textiles, and crafts.

The residents who worked in Acre Steel City engaged in many wild-cat strikes in order to force management to reconsider production cuts and also to improve wages and working conditions. Sephardi-Orientals came to dominate the works committees, and they formed an anti-establishment movement that threatened

European Jewish domination within the factory and within Acre's Labor Federation. They were brought into power in the Labor Federation in order to prevent them from going over to the Nationalist parties, which began to sponsor a labor union movement. The expansion of industry during the second decade of development permitted a larger working-class immigration and it benefited service groups as well. But the middle classes felt that the environment over-emphasized apartment housing and institutional services for the workers. Many moved to Naharya and other garden suburbs in order to carry on life styles more compatible with their tastes.

The Arab minority condemned the government for using national security arguments to deny them employment in Acre Steel City and similar plants. They claimed that Jewish immigrants were benefiting and that prejudice and discrimination were at the heart of the matter. Government and Labor Federation officials told the Arabs that there was sufficient employment for them in construction and that small businesses such as repair shops were receiving subsidy and encouragement as cooperatives. Arabs who were generally unskilled and were fully employed did not remonstrate, but those with technical and clerical skills were especially bitter, for they saw this policy of exclusion extended to employment in offices and other desirable places.

INTERGROUP RELATIONS AT THE WOLFSON HOUSING ESTATE

The Wolfson Housing Estate in Acre's New City inadvertently became a showplace for intergroup relations among Arab and Jewish families. The project dates back to the late 1960s, when the Municipality sought to improve housing in order to enable immigrants to leave the inadequate and crowded quarters of earlier periods. Government ministry officials were in contact with the British Zionist industrialist and philanthropist, Sir Isaac Wolfson, and they persuaded him of the significance of a housing development in Acre. He made a major financial contribution to an apartment complex for 500 families, with small shops and meeting places on the ground floor. The city planners recommended locating the Wolfson Housing Estate in a field that was to become the center for the developed city. This location served as a connector between northern and eastern immigrant quarters and the Mandate New City with its Arab-style housing and modernized shopping district. It was assumed that most new residents would be Sephardi-Orientals and that their social and cultural life would be encouraged by ample apartment space, recreational areas, a kindergarten, and a small chapel. Many families were relocated from transient camps and other deteriorated housing, and they were very much pleased with their new situation.

In the meantime the crisis of Arab housing surfaced in a manner that required immediate attention. Ever since the 1948 exodus of most of Acre's native Arab population, the abandoned housing in the Old City and the Mandate New City had serviced Arab refugees and Jewish immigrants alike. As the government subsidized the construction of new quarters for the Jews, the Arabs were able to spread into the remaining housing in the Old City. However, due to their high birth rate, conditions were more crowded than ever. Young Arabs who were employed in construction work and in other gainful occupations desired to move to more modern housing and they resented the fact that these developments in the New City were for Jews only. The government claimed that Jewish immigrant housing was subsidized through Jewish philanthropic sources: they urged the Arabs to pressure their foundations to invest in housing. But the executors of the *waqf* claimed that they were authorized to sponsor religious and welfare projects and that they were trustees for those Arabs of Acre who were now refugees outside the country. From the 1950s until the mid-1960s, young Arabs pooled family resources to purchase Oriental-style houses and apartments in the Mandate New City from Jews who had occupied them after the Arab-Israeli War and who now desired modern housing in Acre or in the suburbs. Despite this improvement, the Arabs were embittered by the fact that this property had belonged to the Arabs and that the profits were going to Jews. Negotiations for housing on Arab land with government subsidy failed, though individual young families were given the opportunity of moving into selected apartments in immigrant quarters north of the city.

Concerted Arab political action on housing came during the mid-1960s, when winter rains caused a roof in the Old City to collapse and kill an elderly occupant. The family took refuge in Jazzar Mosque, where it attracted the attention of Arab nationalists and the press. Communists actually fought with Laborites within the courtyard of the mosque as they pressed for a resolution to the housing problem for Acre's Arabs. The moderates admonished their colleagues in the Municipality that they would forfeit Arab allegiance to the coalition. The Jewish representatives cited the plight of their own immigrants still living in transient camps on the outskirts of the city. Jewish nationalists pointed out that the Arabs refused to invest their own funds in additional housing. Behind many an argument was the fear by religious parties that inter-marriage would take place if Arab and Jew lived in the same apartment complexes.

Nevertheless, the coalition pressured the Ministry of Housing for an allocation of one apartment per residential block for young Arab families in the new Wolfson Housing Estate. The authorities would take over their present apartments in the Old City and would turn them over to older Arab families who were in need of better housing. The Municipality could then demolish unsound structures, thereby providing space for recreation. The selection of the young Arab families brought accusations of political favoritism from both Arab and Jewish critics. Sephardi-Oriental Jews declared that they would not live together with Arabs. But the authorities remained firm in their plan and the apartments were occupied with little incident. Most Jews behaved correctly and both groups tried to prevent fights among children. Neighbor interaction was strongest within ethnic groupings, but hospitality was extended especially during family celebrations and festivals, according to tradition. The process toward Arab-Jewish accommodation and even integration was proceeding well until international tensions threatened the experiment altogether.

The 1967 War caused a major setback in local Arab-Jewish intergroup relations. During the tense prewar period in May, the Jews feared that the Arabs would seek revenge for previous wrongs and they claimed that the Arabs were acting in an overconfident and insolent manner. The Arabs sensed Jewish hostility and they felt isolated in the new housing areas. Most Arabs took shelter with relatives in the Old City behind the walls, as they did not know what the outcome would be. After their victory in the Six-Day War, the Jews had mixed feelings about whether it would be better for Arabs to be segregated in their own isolated sections or for them to live among Jews, under surveillance. The Arabs became extremely reluctant to live in Jewish neighborhoods. They refused to accept plans proposed for tourist promotion, which would relocate them from the Old City to northern Jewish immigrant quarters. Although most Arabs returned to their apartments in the Wolfson Housing Estate where they enjoy excellent housing, their lives are affected by circumstances beyond local control.

INTERGENERATIONAL INTEGRATION THROUGH THE FORTRESS PRISON MUSEUM

The Jews of Acre have been able to identify more positively with the city since the fortress prison museum has linked Acre's history to the Zionist movement. During the periods of Hellenism, the Crusades, and Turkish and Arab rule, the city had a reputation for hostility to Jewish survival. After the Israeli War of Independence in 1948, the veterans' association of the Jewish Nationalist underground sought permission to establish a Museum for Heroes and Martyrs in the hanging room and adjacent cells of the former British prison for Palestine, located in the old Turkish citadel. The government, which was dominated by Labor, acquiesced to the museum but insisted the Nationalists share the site with a mental hospital for the chronically ill. This was justified by the government as an emergency health situation and also as a new source of employment, e.g., as attendants, for local residents in Acre. The Nationalists felt this was neither a real nor a valid reason and accused the Labor parties of political motives. They called upon all Jews to support the museum and to press for an expansion into the entire citadel complex.

The value of the Nationalist museum as an asset to the image of Acre was realized by local youths, the Nationalist party, tourist interests, and the national press. Young people of Acre reported that they were ridiculed by outsiders for living in a city of "Arabs and crazy people." The Nationalist party accused the coalition of vindictiveness and lack of patriotism. Groups urging improved tourism and the press condemned the government for allowing the mental hospital to continue over two decades on a site so important for visitors. The Religious parties expressed sympathy with the goals of the museum, and when they got control of the Ministry of Health they promised to remove the hospital. Objections by the Marxist Labor party (which controlled the attendants' union) were overcome by offering plans for transferring the workers to other nearby health facilities.

The coalition government ultimately approved the development of the museum as an instrument for unifying the Jewish population within the city and as showing the city's prominent place in Jewish nationalism. Sephardi-Oriental members of the government did not share the partisanship of Labor against the Nationalist party, and the youth were quite sympathetic to the strong anti-Arab reputation of the right-wing party. The Acre Municipality cooperated with the veterans' association of the Nationalists by agreeing to change the names of several streets in the vicinity of the fortress-prison in memory of Nationalists who had been hanged by the British. Sephardi-Orientals were prominent in the ceremonies and this gave them a new identity both with the city and with the Zionist cause.

The hospital was phased out by the early 1970s so that the museum now dominates the citadel. Busloads bring school children and tourists to the museum and they are shown the details of the incarceration and heroic deaths of several young persons with whom they can readily identify in the present era. The book and the movie *Exodus* are well known to foreign visitors, and they ask to see the site of the famous escape of underground militants from the prison, over the adjacent rooftops of Jazzar's bathhouse and the mosque.

There is no attempt to involve Acre's Arabs in the fortress prison museum and division continues to widen between the Jewish and Arab youth of the city. Jewish youth are able to feel an identification with the city through its role in a movement that destroyed British and Arab power. The cause of the Palestinians has gained adherents among the Arab youth of Acre and its district, especially since the 1967 War, and visits with relatives on the occupied West Bank of the Jordan River. Violence has escalated as Arabs seek to rescue their land while intergroup relations between local Jews and Arabs are subject to great stress.

DEVELOPMENT PLANS FOR THE SEAPORT

It is the purpose of the Old Acre Development Corporation to discover and to display the relics of Acre's history in the promotion of tourism. Appropriate government ministries have undertaken surveys, particularly of Crusader sites, to create a "living museum." Archaeological teams have come on the scene in search of the original location of Acre's port. The Ministry of Tourism wishes also to promote modern sports and recreation activities in a sheltered section of the harbor. The Ministries of Transportation and Agriculture have responded to the demands of Acre's Arab fishermen for a breakwater and improvement of jetties and other facilities to increase their catch.

Alongside the port the Khan al-Umdan (Inn of the Columns), which long ago housed Turkish caravans, has been converted into an open-air theatre with plans for hotel rooms above. The harbor mosque and the cafes still serve local Arab needs, but they have increasingly begun to attract persons whose livelihoods and aspirations are associated with visitors to the city. Many of these visitors are legitimate tourists, but others are engaged in unsavory pursuits such as hashish smuggling and espionage, and the police are constantly on the alert.

The Old City of Acre has attracted both romantics and realists who are critical of development plans. Many professional as well as amateur artists came to Acre after the 1948 war in order to capture the panorama of the sea and the walls and the Turkish structures. They lived among the diverse and colorful population and founded studios and pensions for other visiting artists. Some artists joined with craftsmen of metal and wood to promote businesses for the tourist trade. Only a few survived the rigors of bureaucratic controls over licenses and property and the limited number of tourists who would remain in Acre's Oriental surroundings beyond a few hours with the organized tours. The artists helped found the Folklore Museum in Jazzar's famous bathhouse and they sponsored folklore exhibits that featured Arab, Druze, and Turkish customs that are passing away. The government's Department of Antiquities supported the recovery of ancient Canaanite and Hellenistic artifacts and put them on display in the museum. They completed the digging in the Crusaders' Crypt of Saint John. This increased Acre's attraction to organized tour groups and provided a place for concerts in the Knights' Hall. The artists and the promoters of tourism disagree about which relics to preserve and which to convert to more modern purposes.

The Municipality has established a local bureau to provide information about tourist possibilities in Acre and officials are continuously pressuring government ministries and travel corporations to make it possible for the tourists to spend more time in the city. They have responded to newspaper and local public criticism about the lack of adequate overnight accommodations by organizing guestroom services and seeking investors in hotels or motels. There have been several beginnings in hotel construction, but the competition of Naharya seems to be too great. The bulk of tourists want to have their comforts and they are anxious about personal security. Acre is exotic and guided tours are successful, but the Old City appeals mainly to romantics and to persons in search of "adventure." Since the 1967 war, Jerusalem's Holy Places and walled city have been accessible to Israel's tourists, so that Acre's claim to being the most authentic Oriental city in the country has been considerably diminished.

In actuality, the role of tourism in Acre's development is controversial among its residents. The Arabs resent being objects of folklore. They prefer material improvements over the preservation of historical sites. The government has improved housing and sanitation in the Old City by selective demolition and by a comprehensive sewage and indoor plumbing system. Families have, at their own initiative, added rooms on the flat roofs by using discarded stones or concrete block. Much of this work is inconsistent with architectural or historical standards, but it appears to be functional for the overcrowded population. The Municipality is sensitive to safety standards, especially since many structures collapse during storms. But they are also subject to pressures to house a population that is traditional in its culture and fearful of moving too far from its market and other service institutions. The Old Acre Development Corporation is authorized to relocate families from sites that will be developed for purposes of tourism. The process has been extremely slow, not only because of financial reasons, but also because alternative locations have not been found successfully. The 1967 War created such

Arab fishermen making nets.

suspicion between Arabs and Jews that the residents of the Old City have refused to relocate to housing projects where Jews dominate. Rather, the Arabs are gradually purchasing housing in the Mandate New City, which they are fixing according to their means.

The Arabs of Acre's Old City seek government promotion of such traditional enterprises as fishing, crafts, and other small businesses. They use political leverage against the Labor coalition, always threatening to support the Communists or other opposition parties. The fishermen comprise about 300 men and they claim that their need for protection of the harbor has been neglected in favor of Jewish fishermen across the bay in Haifa. After many years, on the eve of elections, the

Labor-sponsored Ministries of Transportation and Agriculture and the Muncipality coalition dedicated a breakwater. The ceremonies included Arab and Jewish men seated by the quay while kerchiefed Arab women watched from the wall above and scouts marched in with bugles and drums. The officials spoke of their support of fishing in Acre and reminded the assembled of their efforts on their behalf. Huge boulders were trucked from the Galilee during the following weeks, and a breakwater emerged to create a lagoon for the fishermen's boats and perhaps for a marina in the future. Officials hoped that the fishermen would show gratitude to the Labor party and to the state of Israel. They worried about possible further incidents in which fishermen from Acre might meet with agents from Egypt and other enemies of the Jewish Homeland. At the fishermen's cafe, the Arab youths of Acre continued to listen to broadcasts from Arab countries and they thought about the Palestinian movement. Visitors commented on the atmosphere of intrigue at the port area where hashish was being exchanged and plots of great importance to the Israeli secret police were being made.

The priorities attached to the development of Acre's Old City vary with ethnic and class interests and cosmopolitan perspectives. Municipality officials recognize the advantages of government ministry inputs for the development of tourism and the preservation of historic sites. They seek to improve the image of the city in order to halt the exodus of the middle class and to encourage investment. They cooperate with Rotary Club attempts to promote Acre's history both for tourism and to create local feeling among the city's youth. But all groups recognize that industry and technology form a more viable base for the city's economic development and that tourism is ancillary. Arabs and Jews, youth and investors alike, favor the noise of the factory and the sight of smoke spiraling into the Mediterranean horizon. The struggle of artists, archaeologists, and persons who value historical and aesthetic considerations is supported only by national newspapers and some local residents.

THE FUNCTIONS OF COMMUNITY

The present-day evidence of trends toward community in Acre are consistent with Middle Eastern historical patterns. Here we find a locality-based service area with a diverse population. Loyalties are derived from common ethnic and class interests and only secondarily from place of residence or livelihood in the city. It is perhaps an urban characteristic to find so much change in the composition of the population and its leadership over time. The rise and fall of cities like Acre have come at the whim of international events.

Within the city there is struggle for personal and for group objectives. External policies are reflected in local programs that generate response and evaluation according to the degree to which they meet the needs of people. The viability of the city is determined by the effectiveness of its essential services. In its daily life the diverse population works together to provide and to utilize these services, such as security, shelter, employment, training, the exchange of goods and the provision

Mandate New City.

for health and the general welfare. Rounds of family celebrations and communal festivals provide for social and spiritual renewal. A civic sense derives from the delivery of these services meeting personal and group interests. It affects officials and residents who are concerned primarily with the city's future. Visitors reinforce the linkage with the past.

The development of Acre, Israel, is a response to national policies and local endeavor. Consensus has emerged as the people of Acre realize that they are in competition with other development towns for national largesse. Such local groups as the Rotary Club, the municipal orchestra, soccer teams, and the sponsors of artistic festivals have brought the public together and have attempted to make the city attractive to outsiders. They supplement the efforts of the political parties, the Labor Federation, and religious groups whose activities pervade the city's institutions and influence its cultural atmosphere.

There are deep cleavages among the ethnic and class groups in Acre and this has limited the city's appeal among its residents. Those who are alienated must be served or else controlled or even expelled. Middle Eastern Jews seem to have found great opportunities for a satisfying family life in Acre. They have been introduced to modern technical production and democratic political institutions as ways for meeting their needs. European Jews have found refuge in Acre, but their children require a more metropolitan environment which may be better satisfied by the resources of the Haifa Bay area. Rural Arabs have obtained basic economic opportunities in Acre, but the middle classes are unable to cope with discrimination against them in technical and clerical pursuits. Israeli culture is, increasingly, a complex of military, industrial, and welfare institutions and the city of Acre serves it as a district service center within the Haifa Bay metropolitan area. Residents who are pragmatic about what the city of Acre is able to provide are most likely to accommodate their personal interests with public goals. These observations are based on a quarter century of Acre in Israel and the response of its people to internal and external events.

APPENDIX A

Selected Chronology Influencing the History of Acre

Historical Period	Major Events Influencing Acre
Stone Age (20,000–4000 B.C.)	
Stone-Bronze Age (4000–3000 B.C.) (Chalcolithic)	
Bronze Age (3000–1200 B.C.) (Canaanite Period)	Ancient Egyptians Execration Records: Tutmis III (1479 B.C.), Amenhotep IV (1375 B.C.), Seti I (1314 B.C.), Rameses II (1288 B.C.)
Iron Age (1200–300 B.C.)	Israelite Tribe of Asher fails to conquer Acre (1250 B.C.)
(Israelite Period)	King David (1006 B.C.)
	King Solomon (968 B.C.)
	Acre conquered by Assyrians (628 B.C.)
	Babylonians destroy First Temple in Jerusalem (587 B.C.)
Babylonian and Persian Period (587–333 B.C.)	Babylonian Exile (587–537 B.C.)
	Acre a Persian base vs. Egypt (526 B.C., 374 B.C.)
Hellenistic Period (332–167 B.C.)	Conquered by Alexander the Great (332 B.C.)
	Called Ptolemais after Egyptian Ptolemy II (281 B.C.)
	Conquered by Antiochus III Seleucid (219 B.C.)
Hasmonean (Maccabean) Period (167–37 B.C.)	Simon (164 B.C.), Jonathan (143 B.C.), Alexander Janai conquered by Ptolemy (103 B.C.)
Roman Period (63 B.C.–395 A.D.)	Conquest by Pompey (63 B.C.)
	Visit by Julius Caesar (48 B.C.), Herod (39 B.C.)
	Jewish revolts against Rome (66–73 A.D.)
	Destruction of Second Temple and Jerusalem (70 A.D.)—beginning of Diaspora (Jewish Dispersion)
	Spread of Christianity (2d and 3d centuries A.D.)

124   THE WALLS OF ACRE

Byzantine (Christian) Rule (395–638 A.D.)	Muhammad's Flight (Hijra) in Arabia (622 A.D.)
Arab-Muslim Rule (638–1099 A.D.)	Arab conquest by Mu'awiya from Damascus (638 A.D.)
	Ahmad ibn Tulun rules from Egypt (871 A.D.)
Crusader Period (1099–1291 A.D.)	Conquest under King Baldwin I (1104 A.D.)
	Visit of Maimonides (The Rambam) (1165 A.D.)
	Visit of Benjamin of Metudellah (1170 A.D.)
	Conquered by Saladdin (1187 A.D.)
	Recaptured by Richard the Lion-hearted (1191 A.D.)
	Visit of Marco Polo (1279 A.D.)
Mamluk Period (1291–1515 A.D.)	Conquest and Destruction by Mamluks (1291 A.D.)
	Expulsion of Jews from Spain (1492 A.D.)—seek refuge in Palestine
Turkish Period (1516–1917 A.D.)	Conquest by Turks via Syria (1516 A.D.)
	Druze Ruler Fakhr ed-Din (1650 A.D.)
	Bedouin Governor Daher el 'Omar (1740 A.D.)
	Governor Ahmed el-Jazzar (1775–1804 A.D.)
	Siege by Napoleon Bonaparte (1799 A.D.)
	Suleiman Pasha (1804–1819 A.D.)
	'Abdullah Pasha (1819–1831 A.D.)
	Conquest by Ibrahim 'Ali from Egypt (1831–1839 A.D.)
	Reconquest by Turks and Allies (1840 A.D.)
	Balfour Declaration (Nov. 2, 1917)
British Mandate (1918–1948)	Captured by British under Allenby (1918)
	Acre Fortress made into Central Prison (1920)
	Arab-Jewish Riots (1921, 1929, 1936–1939)
	British White Paper restricting Zionist work in Palestine (1939)
	Haifa Port a military supply base during World War II (1939–1945)
	United Nations Partition Resolution for Palestine (Nov. 29, 1947)

Israeli Statehood (1948–)	Proclamation of State of Israel (May 14, 1948)
	Acre occupied by Haganah (May 16–18, 1948)
	Acre Municipality established (May 25, 1949)
	National and local elections (1949, 1951, 1955, 1959, 1965, 1969, 1973)
	Sinai Campaign (1956)
	Six-Day War (June, 1967)
	Yom Kippur War (Oct. 1973)

APPENDIX B

Voting for the Israeli National Assembly and the Acre Municipal Council 1969 and 1973

Major Political Parties	Vote for Israeli National Assembly Vote in Israel (percent) 1969	1973	Vote in Acre (percent) 1969	1973	Vote for Acre Municipal Council (percent) 1969	1973
Labor Alignment and Affiliates	54	45	54	41	54	59
National Religious Parties	14	12	18	12	15	10
Nationalist Alliance	26	34	14	28	14	11
New Communists	2	3	7	15	7	11
Others	4	6	7	4	10	9

ANALYSIS: The Labor Alignment and its Arab and other affiliates gained a plurality of votes in Israel and in Acre during both the 1969 and 1973 elections. But the vote for the Labor Alignment in the National Assembly was greatly reduced due to criticism about the conduct of the recent war. The Nationalist Alliance gained votes among Jews and the New Communists gained votes among Arabs. Nevertheless, due to local leadership circumstances, the Labor Alignment and its Arab affiliates remained quite strong in Acre Municipal Council elections. National Religious Parties, which usually join in the governing Coalition, showed slight declines in 1973. This implies that the young voting population has become more secular and it supports either Labor or else Jewish or Arab nationalist alternatives.

APPENDIX C

Selective Population Facts: City of Acre

	Turkish Period[a] (1890's)	British Mandate Period[b] (1922)	(1944)	Israel Period[c] (1948)	(1973)
Total	10,400	6,420	12,300	4,000	35,000
Muslim	6,780	4,883	9,900	2,000	6,000
Sunni	6,500				
Shi'a	280				
Christian	2,744	1,344	2,300	1,000	2,000
Orthodox	2,000	846			
Greek Cath.	555	276			
Latin Cath.	139	71			
Maronite	50	46			
Anglican	0	74			
Jews	766	78	0	1,000	27,000
Foreign and Others	110	115			

[a] Turkish Government statistics reported by Vital Cuinet, 1896, *Syrie, Liban et Palestine* (Paris: Ernest Leroux).
[b] Department of Statistics, Government of Palestine.
[c] Estimates from Municipality and newspapers. See following Table for more exact Israeli Government Statistics. Population has grown slowly since 1965.

POPULATION GROWTH DURING PERIOD OF
INTENSIVE IMMIGRATION: CITY OF ACRE*

Jun. 1948	3,300
Nov. 1948	4,016
Dec. 1950	12,200
Dec. 1952	16,600
Dec. 1955	19,200
May 1961	25,222
Dec. 1965	32,300
Dec. 1966	32,400
Dec. 1970	33,900
Dec. 1971	34,200

* *Statistical Abstract of Israel*, 1972.

Glossary

(A) Arabic (H) Hebrew (T) Turkish (Y) Yiddish

al- (A): Prefix "the"
Aliyah Noar (H): Immigrant Youth organization
'Am Yisrael (H): Israeli or Jewish People
araq (A): anise liquor
Argaman (H): purple (ref. dye)
Ashkenazi (H): Germany; European Jew
baal (H): Master (e.g., Canaanite deity)
Bahai: International religious group originating in Iran
baqlava (T): sesame-honey pastry
bar mitzvah (H): confirmation of son
bat (H): daughter
bedouin (A): nomadic tribesman
ben (H): son
bint am (A): patrilineal parallel cousin for marriage
bogruth (H): university entrance examination
Caliphate (A): "successor" to Muhammed; Muslim empire
Capitulations: European treaty enclaves in Turkish Empire
chaim (H): Life
challah (Y): braided Sabbath bread
cholent (Y): Sabbath meat-bean casserole
Cohen (H): priest (highest status)
debka (A): Arab line dance
Diaspora: Lands of Jewish Dispersion from Palestine or Israel
Druze: Near Eastern sect derived from Islam
effendi (T): civilian title for landowner
el- (A): Prefix "the"
Eretz Yisrael (H): The Land of Israel
felafel (A): fried chickpea paste balls
fellah (A): farmer, peasant
Gadna (H): secondary school military training organization
gazoz: "eau gaseuse"—soda
gefulte (Y): filled or stuffed (fish)
Gentile: Non-Jew
Greek fire: Like napalm, pitch
Hagadah (H): Narrative of Israelite Exodus from Egypt
Haganah (H): Israeli Defense Forces
Hajj (A): Pilgrimage (to Mecca)
hammam (A): bathhouse

hamuula (A): clan, extended family
Hanukkah (H): "Dedication" of Temple after defeat of Hellenists by Maccabees
Hatiqvah (H): "Hope," Zionist and Israel national anthem
Hellenism: Greek culture spread by Alexander the Great
Herut (H): Freedom, a Jewish Nationalist political party
Histadrut (H): General Labor Federation
hora (H): Israeli circle dance
Hospitaler: Crusader order providing shelter
humus (A): chickpea paste salad
ibn (A): son
'Id al-Adha (A): Festival of the Sacrifice (associated with the Pilgrimage)
'Id al-Fitr (A): Festival of Fast-Breaking at the end of Ramadan
-im (H); *-in* (A): Plural suffix
Irgun Zvei Leumi (I.Z.L.) (H): Jewish Nationalist underground fighters
Islam (A): "Submission" to religion of 'Allah as One God and Muhammed as His Messenger
kadish (H): Mourning (prayer), Sanctification
Karaite (H): Jewish sect refusing to accept rabbinical commentaries as sacred
kfar (H); *kufr* (A): village
khan (T): inn, caravansarei
khoury (A): priest
kibbutz (H): agricultural commune
kidush (H): blessing over wine
Knesseth (H): Israel National Assembly
Koran (Quran): Muslim Holy Book
kufiya (A): men's headcloth
Kupat Holim (H): Sick Fund of Histadrut
Ladino (H): Judaeo-Spanish language
Lag b'Omer (H): 30 days to counting barley harvest between Passover and Shavuoth (Feast of Weeks); Commemorates Jewish rebellion against the Romans
lebaniye (A): soured milk, like yogurt
Levant (A): Eastern Mediterranean coastal region, including Syria and Lebanon and northern Palestine
levantine: alluding to superficial acquisition of western culture on a Near Eastern base
Likud: National Alliance for 1973 elections
Maghrib (A): West (ref. North Africa)
Mamluk (T): Slave group that overcame Crusader Kingdom
MAPAI (H): Labor Party
MAPAM (H): Marxist Labor Party
Maronite: Uniate (Roman Catholic) group dominant in Lebanon
matzah (H): unleavened bread
mellah (A): Jewish quarter in Arab city
menorah (H): candelabrum featured at Hanukkah
mohar (A): bride-price
millet (T): minority group participation in the larger society
Mizrahi (H): easterner, Oriental; also Israeli Religious party
muezzin (A): calls the Muslim Faithful to prayer
Muslim: Believer in 'Allah as One God and Muhammed as His Messenger
noblesse oblige: patronage obligation
Passover, Pesah (H): Feast of Israelite Exodus from Egypt
pitta (A): flat bread (with envelope)
proteksia: political or bureaucratic favoritism

Purim (H): "Lots"—Jewish festival commemorating Queen Esther and the Persian experience.
qadi (A): religious judge at Shari'a court
Qur'an (See Koran) (A): Muslim Holy Book
Ramadan (A): month for fasting by Muslims
Rosh Hashanah (H): New Year
sabra (H): "cactus fruit," native-born Israeli Jew
seder (H): Passover meal
seker (H): examination for secondary school matriculation
Sephardi (H): Jew from Spain, Mediterranean area
shalom (H): Peace, a greeting
shashliq (A): skewered meat
Shavuoth (H): Feast of Weeks
sheikh (A): an elder (to be honored)
Shi'a (A): Muslim denomination found in Iran; also various cult or sect groups in other Middle East countries
shikun (H): a housing development
Simchat Torah (H): Festival, Rejoicing in the Law
Succoth (H): Thanksgiving Festival of Tabernacles
Sunni (A): Major Muslim denomination found in the Levant, Egypt, and Arabia.
suq (A): market, street of stalls
synagogue: Jewish house of worship
tallith (H): prayer shawl worn by men at Jewish religious services
tel (A): mound, hillock
Templar: Crusader military order providing escort
tephillin (H): phylacteries, or leather bound boxes with prayers enclosed; worn by men on head and arms during daily morning prayer services
Torah (H): Pentateuch, Five Books of Moses, Law
tsadakah (H): charity
ulpan (H): intensive Hebrew study group
umma (A): people, nation
waqf (A): Muslim charitable foundation
yarmulke (Y): skullcap
yeshivah (Y): religious academy
Yiddish (Y): Judeao-German language
Yom Kippur (H): Day of Atonement
zaka (A): almsgiving
Zionism (H): Jewish national movement

Recommended reading

COMMUNITY AND URBAN STUDIES

Adams, Robert McC., 1966. *The Evolution of Urban Society.* Chicago: Aldine. Comparative analysis of urban cultural development in Mesopotamia and Prehispanic Mexico, with emphasis on transition from theocratic to political control as expanding states.

Breese, Gerald, ed., 1969. *The City in Newly Developing Countries.* Englewood Cliffs, N.J.: Prentice-Hall. Worldwide regional coverage of urbanism and urbanization process including institutional functions and demographic aspects.

Gluckman, Max, ed., 1964. *Closed Systems and Open Minds.* Chicago: Aldine. Systemic anthropological approach to tribal and village symbolism and interrelationships and to urban and industrial networks.

Redfield, Robert, 1955. *The Little Community.* Chicago: University of Chicago Press. Describes the extent to which community is a microcosm and representative of something beyond itself.

Richardson, Miles, 1970. *San Pedro, Colombia: Small Town in a Developing Society,* New York: Holt, Rinehart and Winston. Case study of the relations and functions of small town structure, institutions, and people in larger societal context.

Sjoberg, Gideon, 1960. *The Preindustrial City.* Glencoe, Ill.: Free Press. Emphasizes similarities in development, institutionalization, structure, and functions in historical dimension.

MEDITERRANEAN AND MIDDLE EAST STUDIES

Berger, Morroe, 1962. *The Arab World Today.* New York: Doubleday. Arab and Muslim history, personality, social institutions, and social change as a regional and cultural approach.

Coon, Carleton S., 1959. *Caravan: The Story of the Middle East.* New York: Holt, Rinehart and Winston. Major cultural and subcultural groups, functions of Islam, settlement types, and symbiosis.

Gulick, John, 1967. *Tripoli: A Modern Arab City.* Cambridge, Mass.: Harvard University Press. Comprehensive description and analysis of Lebanese coastal city in cultural, personal, and world perspective.

Halpern, Manfred, 1963. *The Politics of Social Change in the Middle East and North Africa.* Princeton: Princeton University Press. Analysis of the causes and characteristics of regional revolution through forces, groups, ideas, and institutions.

Lapidus, Ira M., 1967. *Muslim Cities in the Later Middle Ages.* Cambridge, Mass.: Harvard University Press. Social and political life in the Mamluk Empire, especially Damascus, Aleppo, and Cairo.

Lapidus, Ira M., ed., 1969. *Middle Eastern Cities.* Berkeley and Los Angeles: University of California Press. Symposium contrasts ancient, Islamic, and contemporary Middle Eastern urbanism.

Lerner, Daniel, 1958. *The Passing of Traditional Society.* New York: Free Press. Attitudinal survey in several countries measuring transition from traditional to modern values.

Levy, Reuben, 1965. *The Social Structure of Islam.* Cambridge, England: Cambridge University Press. Comprehensive analysis of institutional forms based on Islamic religious pronouncements and historical practices.

Longrigg, Stephen H., 1963. *The Middle East: A Social Geography.* Chicago: Aldine. Regional, historical, and contemporary sociocultural and institutional analysis.

Peristiany, J. G., ed., 1968. *Contributions to Mediterranean Sociology.* Paris and The Hague: Mouton. Social values, village structure, patron-client relations, migration, social change, and economic development prerequisites.

Pitt-Rivers, Julian, ed., 1963. *Mediterranean Countrymen.* Paris and The Hague: Mouton. Social anthropology of village and city life, values, status, power, and change.

Sweet, Louise E., ed., 1970. *Peoples and Cultures of the Middle East,* 2 vols. New York: The Natural History Press (and Doubleday). Ecological and cultural diversity, settlement patterns, institutions, daily life, and change.

ISRAEL

Atiya, Aziz, 1962. *Crusade, Commerce and Culture.* New York: Wiley (Science Editions for Indiana University Press). Contrasts the Crusades and their impact on the region and the relationship of Arab culture to the West in the Middle Ages.

Ben-Ami, Aharon, 1969. *Social Change in a Hostile Environment: The Crusaders' Kingdom of Jerusalem.* Princeton: Princeton University Press. Intersocietal relations, historical interlockage, institutional lag and innovative functions, critical turning points, leadership roles, and conflict systems.

Cohen, Abner, 1965. *Arab Border-Villages in Israel.* Manchester, England: Manchester University Press. Impact of Isareli situation on economy, power and prestige, clan and village unity, and conflict under border conditions.

Eisenstadt, Shmuel N., 1967. *Israeli Society.* New York: Basic Books. Comprehensive historical, structural, institutional, and cultural analysis, citing many local sources in depth.

Fein, Leonard J., 1968. *Israeli Politics and People.* Boston: Little, Brown. Historical analysis of power and policy formation and exercise.

Landau, Jacob M., 1969. *The Arabs in Israel: A Political Study.* London: Oxford University Press. Modes of cultural and political adaptation and analysis of elections and leadership.

Michener, James A., 1965. *The Source.* New York: Random House. Fictional history of the northern district from prehistoric to contemporary times, captures the flavor of each epoch and utilizes true incidents to make basic points about indigenous and invading peoples and cultures.

Patai, Raphael, 1953; 2d rev. ed., 1970*. *Israel between East and West.* Philadelphia: Jewish Publication Society. Analysis of historical culture-contact situation and consequences for each group in crises and change.

Shuval, Judith T., 1963. *Immigrants on the Threshold.* New York: Atherton Press. Attitudinal survey of social distance among Jewish immigrants living in Israel.

Uris, Leon, 1958. *Exodus.* New York: Doubleday. Fictionalized story of the Zionist movement and the establishment of the state of Israel. Covers the feelings of veterans and immigrants and features the prison break in Acre.

Weingrod, Alex, 1966. *Reluctant Pioneers: Village Development in Israel.* Ithaca, N.Y.: Cornell University Press. Acculturation problems of Moroccan Jewish immigrants sent to cooperative agricultural villages in Israel.

Willner, Dorothy, 1969. *Nation-Building and Community in Israel.* Princeton: Princeton University Press. Analysis of land settlement policy and programs by which Moroccan Jews accommodate to Israeli institutions.

* This edition was published in Westport, Conn., by Greenwood Press.

Additional references

THEORETICAL SOURCES

Arensberg, Conrad, and Solon T. Kimball, 1965. *Culture and Community*. New York: Harcourt.
Bernard, Jessie, 1962. *American Community Behavior*. New York: Holt, Rinehart and Winston.
Buckley, Walter, ed., 1968. *Modern Systems Research for the Behavioral Scientist*. Chicago: Aldine.
Clark, Terry, ed., 1968. *Community Structure and Decision-Making*. San Francisco: Chandler Publishing Company.
Demerath, Nicholas J., III, and Richard A. Peterson, eds., 1967. *System, Change and Conflict*. New York: Free Press.
Doxiadis, Constantinos A., 1968. *Ekistics*. New York: Oxford University Press.
Etzioni, Amitai, 1968. *The Active Society*. New York: Free Press.
Parsons, Talcott, et al., 1961. *Theories of Society*, 2 vols. New York: Free Press.
Rose, Arnold M., ed., 1962. *Human Behavior and Social Processes*. Boston: Houghton Mifflin.
Sanders, Irwin T., 1966. *The Community*. New York: Ronald.
Strauss, Anselm, ed., 1968. *The American City*. Chicago: Aldine.
Wallace, Walter L., 1969. *Sociological Theory*. Chicago: Aldine.
Warren, Ronald L., ed., 1966; rev. ed., 1973. *Perspectives on the American Community*. Chicago: Rand McNally.
Zollschan, George K., and Walter Hirsch, eds., 1964. *Explorations in Social Change*. Boston: Houghton Mifflin.

ISRAEL AND ACRE

Cuinet, Vital, 1896. *Syrie, Liban et Palestine*. Paris: Ernest Leroux.
Dichter, Bernard, 1973. *The Maps of Acre*. Municipality of Acre, Israel.
ESCO Foundation for Palestine, Inc., 1947. *Palestine: A Study of Jewish, Arab, and British Policies*, 2 vols. New Haven: Yale University Press.
Herzl, Theodore, 1902, 1960. *Old-New Land*. Haifa: Haifa Publishing Company.
Kesten, A., 1963. *Acre, The Old City: Survey and Planning*. Jerusalem: Prime Minister's Office.
Makhouly, Na'im, and C. N. Johns, 1946. *Guide to Acre*. Jerusalem: Government of Palestine Department of Antiquities.
Municipality of Acre, 1968. *Twentieth Anniversary of Acre in Israel* (Hebrew).

Orni, Efraim, and Elisha Efrat, 1964; 3d rev. ed., 1972*. *Geography of Israel.* Jerusalem: Israel. (Program for Scientific Translation)
Spiegel, Erika, 1967. *New Towns in Israel.* New York: Praeger.
Vilnay, Zev, 1965. *The Guide to Israel.* Jerusalem: Silvan Press.
Vilnay, Zev, 1968. *The Changing Face of Acco.* Acre: Tambour Paints (Hebrew).
Vilnay, Zev, 1968. *The New Israel Atlas.* Jerusalem: Israel Universities Press.
Israel Government. *Yearbook.* Jerusalem: Israel Government Press.

* This edition was published in New York by American Heritage Publishing Company, Inc.